The Ultimate Hand Book

SELF-CARE FOR BODYWORKERS
AND MASSAGE THERAPISTS

THE ULTIMATE HAND BOOK:

SELF-CARE FOR BODYWORKERS
AND MASSAGE THERAPISTS

Maja Evans, D.H., C.M.T.
834 41st Avenue, San Francisco, CA 94121
(415)221-5530

Photography: Photos by Vera, Mill Valley and Greg Harning, San Anselmo, CA.
Cover Illustration: Deborah Harvey, Corte Madera, CA.
Illustrations in Book: Maja Evans, San Francisco, CA.
Typesetting: D D Graphics, Corte Madera, CA and Acorn Graphics, San Rafael, CA.
Chapter six was written with the assistance of Daniel S. Harvey, Director of the Sports Medicine Clinic, Oakland, CA, and Judith Aston of Aston-Patterning,® Incline Village, NV.

Printed in the United States of America.
Laughing Duck Press.
ISBN 0-9632875-0-8

This book is dedicated to Robert,

who made it possible.

Table of Contents

Preface   vi

Statement of Purpose   viii

Acknowledgements   ix

ONE   Burnout   1

TWO   The Dynamics of Burnout   11

THREE The Heart Path   29

FOUR   The Self-Caring Healer   43

FIVE   Developing the Habit of Self-Care   57

SIX   Physical Self-Care   71

SEVEN Psychological Self-Care   99

EIGHT Psychic Self-Care   120

NINE   Abundance   137

TEN   "Success" by Joycelyn Olivier   158

Bibliography   170

**So...you want a career in bodywork.
Welcome to the club.**

As long as you can remember you wanted to be a healer. While you were doing that old job, all you could dream of was right livelihood. You knew you were destined for greater things than shuffling papers, plates, and/or shoveling dirt. You wanted to do something that mattered, to make a contribution to the health and well-being of the planet.

You've invested a lot of time and money in your education. You've got your table, and bought your sheets. You have a space set aside for bodywork. You even have a card with your name and phone number on it. Now you're well on your way to becoming a healer. Congratulations.

Do you realize that 80% of the people who start out in bodywork drop out after the first two years? That a mere 5% ever develop a full-time practice? That the main reason people drop out is burnout? They get frustrated and quit because:

1. They can't get their practice off the ground,
2. Their hands give out,
3. They hate the "sales and marketing" part,
4. They don't have the physical stamina for bodywork,
5. They conclude the world is just not ready for their work.

These are all perfectly good reasons to quit, but it doesn't have to be because of burnout anymore.

This book was written for you so that you know what lies ahead in getting your business off the ground.

A bodywork practice is a business, and many of the same rules apply to a practice as do to any small business. You've done your preparation, now it's time to do your promotion, and that is what makes or breaks a business.

You've got to reach out to everyone you can and let them know you have a service to offer. Then you have to deliver that service conveniently and consistently to your clients. And you have to keep a fresh flow of new people coming in all the time if you want your business to stay afloat.

You also have to be physically, mentally, and emotionally sound because the amount of energy which you give your clients will also make or break you.

For me, starting a bodywork practice was fun, exciting, and challenging, and I am happy to share my journey with you. It hasn't always been easy, but bodywork is so important to me, it's been worth it.

—Maja Evans

Statement of Purpose

If you find yourself getting overextended and "burned out," despite your good intentions to do otherwise, this book is for you. It addresses the various levels of burnout (physical, emotional, psychic, and financial), develops a model of the Self-Caring Healer, and discusses practical ways to deal with the underlying causes of burnout that professionals in caregiving careers often experience. The path to becoming a better healer is full of challenges, surprises, and unexpected outcomes.

This book illuminates the path so that the way is a little easier and lighter. Only you can walk your journey. The best guide, and really the only true guide, is a good heart. Keep the heart clear, because no matter what happens to you, you won't get lost. The doorway to your deepest dream is in the heart.

Acknowledgments

I am infinitely grateful to the many people have helped me over the years with this book. My thanks to Robert Schile, Tom Graves, Joan Nelson, and Nancy Addess who helped me edit the endless reams of material that came out of my prolific computer.

And to the consultants: Judith Aston, Miguel Franco, Joycelyn Olivier, and Dan Harvey.

And to my teachers: Lee Glickstein, Arina Isaacson, Tom Stucker, Stan Russell, and Ellen Serber.

And to Ariana, David, Greg, Anthony, Melissa, Mary, SteveAnne, and Carolyn who inspired me to keep on growing.

...and to Bill who made me laugh.

CHAPTER ONE

BURNOUT
THE OCCUPATIONAL HAZARD OF CAREGIVERS

When I first began to do massage, I worked in spas. An average work day was six people. The hours were long, and the work was very physical, but I enjoyed it. One day a fellow massage therapist turned to me and said, "I don't know about you but I just can't do another body. I'm sick of seeing them, I hate the smell of massage oil, I'm sick of cosmic mush music, and if I have to do another body today, I think I'll die."

This statement really struck me. I was fresh in my career and couldn't believe that something which gave me so much pleasure could give this woman so much boredom and pain. Since then I've experienced bodyworker's burnout in its diverse and multifarious forms. Not only was I burned out, but the subject of burnout came up in discussions with my colleagues again and again.

Many people quit bodywork. Burnout is the most proffered reason for dropping out of the profession. I've wondered why burnout is so prevalent in our profession and began to study it. Out of that research came this book. Essentially, this is what I've found:

1. **Body burnout -** The first things to go are usually the thumbs, but the hands, wrists, forearms, and backs often give out as well.
2. **Financial burnout -** A lot of people drop out because they could not make enough to live on.
3. **Emotional burnout -** Even if the bodyworker gets over the initial obstacles, bodywork profes-

sionals find themselves losing their patience with, interest in, and/or desire to maintain a lively and healthy practice. Why?

The majority of people attracted to bodywork and massage are warm, loving, and generous people. We enjoy caring for others. We love to give.

When we first start out there is boundless love, energy, and willingness to give. Massage is fun, we are learning new things all the time, and people appreciate what we do. After each session we feel peaceful, useful, and energized. As healers, we feel our life has purpose and meaning.

Yet taking care of others has its own peculiar type of stress. All caregivers experience burnout from time to time—home health attendants, nurses and doctors, mothers, etc. The caring profession requires the person to give and give and give, and sometimes there's nothing left over for ourselves.

The greatest weakness of the caregiving personality is that they love to give so much, that they give too much. They give too much of their time, they try to do too much at a time, they take on the responsibility for the health and well-being of everyone around them, and then they take on their problems. In short they abuse their bodies, minds and souls trying to get the people they love happy all the time. Although the client, the patient, the child—whoever is the recipient of our affection and attention—may feel better than before, the caregiver ends up feeling frustrated and drained by the interaction.

Caregivers can give so much so fast for so long that they get drained before they know it, and then they stop enjoying what they do.

It gets to be a vicious cycle, they want to change, but they don't know how to stop. People take advantage of their good nature, and it's not that obvious what they (the caregivers) are doing to help create the situation. Negative feelings arise and begin to affect the quality of their work. They don't get the results they used to. The frustration builds to a crisis—that crash and burn feeling. By this time they've come to the conclusion that there is no use in trying anymore, they can't get the respect and gratitude they deserve. They get discouraged and quit.

Don't let this happen to you. If you are a caregiver, you need **nurturing.** Caregivers have an enormous need for nurturing, and we will explain why in the second chapter of this book. This need for nurturing is what drives us to nurture and care for others. We derive pleasure from giving to others what we would like for ourselves. It is a healthy need, not just for us, but for the world at large.

The best way we can take care of ourselves is to take a break: have a massage, go on vacation, avail ourselves of a type of therapy which helps us to stay emotionally clean, make sure our busy schedule allows for at least one time slot for regeneration every day.

To be an effective and joyous healer, we will need to treat our body as if it were a fine car, like a Porsche or a Rolls Royce. Lavish attention on your body. Feed it good food, wear soft and silky clothes, buy fresh flowers just for you.

The more you love yourself, the more love you have to give.

Wrecked Thumbs, Wracked Backs

Physical burnout can cut your bodywork career short, especially if you have to do a lot of work before you can build strength and stamina. Thumbs, wrists, neck and back are often injured while doing massage. You may feel physically drained at the end of a day if you do a lot of people or have an especially difficult client.

Even though massage is fun, it is still a physical and mental discipline. The time injuries are most likely to happen are when you get tired. Even though you know better than to lean into the table, you get a little punchy and lazy. Then your arms and back take the load instead of your whole body. Maybe there's a tough muscle that just won't yield and you use your thumbs too much. Or you forget to use your center when lifting, and your low back goes out.

If something starts to hurt, stop abusing it. In the chapter on "Physical Self-Care," we will suggest alternate ways to use your body that will protect your joints and prevent burnout. Try them out and see what works for you. Every body is different and has its own unique way of working. Learn how to use yours wisely by educating yourself, and watching tension in your body. Strive always to maximize the efficiency of what you do by developing your understanding of the mechanics of the body.

In addition to paying attention to the mechanics of your movements, it is important to keep your breath flowing. Freeing the breath heightens awareness. This distinct awareness enables you to notice ease in your movements. It is the key to your best work.

Taking Care of Business

Right livelihood includes making enough to live on comfortably. Yet many bodyworkers and massage therapists complain of not making enough to meet the most basic needs.

Bodywork is a business. We have an invaluable service which we provide to clients. They, in turn, are happy to pay us to perform this service for them. If we do our job well, including the business end of it, there is no reason why we should have to worry about money, competition, or staying in the bodywork business.

Promotion and marketing, quality of service, the comfort and professionalism of the place of business, and the volume of repeat business will make or break the bodywork practice.

There are a lot of reasons why people do not make it in business, but the reasons all boil down to three things:

1. Ignorance of basic business practices
2. Lack of focused effort
3. Funds run out before there is a positive cash flow.

Each of these things you can do something about. If you are ignorant, you can educate yourself. If your first efforts do not get the results you want, analyze them and refine them. Don't give up before you've made an honest effort. If you have a negative cash flow, then get money from other sources until you have a positive cash flow—work a second job, sell water filters, get a business loan. The bodywork practice has several advantages over other start-up businesses: comparatively low overhead, self-employment, flexibility, and the emotional satisfaction of helping others feel better.

We believe that success in bodywork is so important that we've devoted two chapters to the subject. The ninth chapter discusses ways you can take care of yourself financially. The tenth chapter is written by Joycelyn Olivier who not only built a highly successful bodywork practice, she also developed a neuromuscular massage form called Conscious Bodywork, founded a professional school for bodyworkers and holistic healers, and brought together the first Somatics Community for body therapists. For more information about Conscious Bodywork, Alive & Well!, or the Somatics Community contact:

Alive & Well!
100 Shaw Drive
San Anselmo, CA 94960
(415)258-0402

Joycelyn Olivier is an inspiration to many people, myself included. She has helped her students to acquire the necessary skills to build successful health practices in a highly competitive marketplace. Her piece is titled "Success."

Emotions

Deeply ingrained but unrealistic standards of excellence drive us to impossible goals. We fall short of our standards and feel guilty because we have failed. Self-defeating cycles of striving, abuse, and failure drive us deeper into our despair.

Learning to accept ourselves just as we are is:

- The first step to achieving satisfaction.
- The second step is to see ourselves as a work in progress.

- The third step is acknowledging our growth and our goodness of heart.

We'll always have ways to improve. Stopping once in a while to appreciate ourselves and how far we've come makes the process more satisfying.

Satisfaction is a feeling. Achievement will not necessarily bring us satisfaction, cultivating the feeling will.

We will continue the cycle of impossible goals and inevitable frustrations unless we acknowledge our true gifts and use them. Then and only then will we experience ourselves at our best.

The role of bodyworker is powerful, but the role of client is more so. The decision to do something about the pain, the decision to call the bodyworker, and the decision to let go and allow the transformation to happen all belong to the client. These three decisions elicit the deepest healing from the bodyworker.

Emotionally it is very tough to be a healer. There is a level of responsibility and authority that is akin to being a demi-god. Our clients are vulnerable because of the intimacy of the bodywork session, and the role of trust in the relationship between client and practitioner is paramount. This is a role that priests, doctors, and scientists once held in our society, but are rapidly losing due to abuses of power and growing distrust in the general population. Many people seeking a better solution to their health problems are turning to the alternative therapies like massage and bodywork.

We have a lot of expectations to deal with in the session. We not only have to deal with our clients' expectations in a compassionate and non-judgmental manner, we also have our own ideals, human drives, and internal conflicts to deal with as well. We have a responsibility as a healer to respond to every client with integrity, and to not abuse our power of authority. There are boundaries around what we can do with bodywork, and for our own protection, and for the protection of our profession, we need to respect these. We will be asked to fill roles we were not meant to fill; we are not doctors, so we are not qualified to offer free medical advice, nor are we priests, psychiatrists, mothers, or lovers. It is important that we be clear about our boundaries. There is a lot of good we can do within our domain.

We know it would be foolish to try to be everything for our clients. The evidence of this is in the numerous malpractice suits which beset the medical profession and which are ruining the health industry. If we can keep reminding ourselves that we are only guides on the path of healing, and not omniscient powers, we can keep our responsibilities in perspective and actually aid people in doing some real healing.

Taking on Negative Energy

There is another unfortunate side effect of healing work which in the profession is often referred to as "taking on the client's negative energy." How does it happen? Are there effective ways to block it? How does one clear toxic energy out of one's system?

One of the most fascinating studies in the transference of illness from a unhealthy person to a healthy person was by a little known scientist, named Mr. Eeman. In his book, <u>Cooperative Healing</u>, Mr. Eeman explains the results of over seventy tests which were made and of the reactions to substances introduced through the energy flow into the body of the subject.

The person volunteering for the test was asked to lie down on a cot and then hooked up to a "relaxation circuit" which was made of insulated copper wire. One of the wires to the circuit was then cut and fastened to two electrodes thrust into vials containing medicine, food, and toxic substances. He found that people reacted to the substances as if they had taken them into their bodies.

In another experiment he hooked up people in series to discover the effect that an unhealthy person might have on a healthy person. He discovered that vital energy flowed from one person to another, particularly when there was a great difference in the level of vital energy between the two people.

Interestingly, what he discovered is that the healthy person would manifest the same symptoms of the unhealthy person as if there were a transfer of bodily poisons. A person suffering from infection and fever, when hooked up in a circuit with a well person, transferred some of his fever and discomfort to him. Equally surprising was his discovery that a person who had recovered from a disease such as typhoid fever, measles or smallpox, and had developed the proper antitoxins in their blood, was a great help to one suffering from the same disease.

The third thing he discovered was the transference of symptoms took place even without the wires. He tried connecting people with strips of cloth, and that worked. Then he removed the cloth connection. He was surprised to discover **the toxicity was still being transferred**, when the healthy person and the ill person were in proximity to each other.[1]

A possible explanation for this phenomenon

comes from the kahunas of Hawaii. They held that all things and substances had "aka" bodies (the etheric body of modern parapsychology). One quality of the aka body is that it sticky, just like a spider's web, and once it makes contact with something it leaves an aka thread behind. Mana (vital energy) flows along this thread, somewhat like electricity flowing through a wire, but it does not disperse in strength over a distance.

It is possible that while touching the client some of your vital energy is being transferred into their body and that some of their negative energy is being transferred into you. If this is the case, then developing a methodology for dealing with the transference would be useful to the healer.

In Chapter Six, titled "Psychic Self-Care," we will discuss some of the more popular methods of cleansing your "aka" body of negative energy.

[1] Long, Max Freedom, Secret Science at Work, Marina del Rey: DeVorss, 1953.

CHAPTER TWO

THE DYNAMICS OF BURNOUT

 Caregivers want to serve mankind, and help others feel better. Taking care of others gives us a feeling of personal value and brings us acknowledgment, recognition, and attention. We like the feeling of being needed.

However, being needed all the time and giving out so much of ourselves can lead to other feelings which are not so pleasant, i.e., being tired, irritable, drained, used, and exploited. Normally we love people, but when we find ourselves just wanting to spend some time alone, we are experiencing "burn-out."

Many of us in service professions often have this problem and are at a loss for how to deal with it. Serving others is as natural for us as breathing and eating. Taking time for ourselves seems "selfish."

Giving ourselves the gift of time is not selfish, it's balancing.

Caregivers are special people and have special needs.

- We have a need to be wanted.
- We have a need to feel productive, useful, even heroic at times, because that helps us feel right about being alive and taking up space on the planet.
- We need to feel good about ourselves. Being in the caring role gives us a feeling that we are a

good person. Being in charge helps us feel confident and in control of the situation even in the face of chaos, violence and death.

- We need order, security, and safety, because we have experienced a lot of chaos.
- We need a lot of love, reassurance, and nurturing.

Security, love, being wanted and needed by another are good feelings to have. They are probably the deepest psychological drives on our path to personal fulfillment.

These are all valid needs, but if we are out of touch with other basic needs, i.e. rest, food, time out, emotional and creative expression, we will not be taking care of ourselves adequately.

First let's take a look at how burnout happens.

D>R➔E

**When Demands exceed Resources,
we experience Exhaustion.**

Solving burnout sounds easy—just balance the equation—but it's not as simple as that. There are hidden factors. Let's look at some of the most common ones.

Responsibility - As caregivers, we habitually take on responsibility, then we are driven by our feelings of guilt to get it all done, and neglect our own needs. We build up a reservoir of buried resentments, hurts, sorrows, and fears.

The bigger this reservoir gets, the harder it is for us to hear our inner selves speak clearly about what we want.

Communication Breakdown - The most unfortunate effect of "burnout" is that the communication between the inner and outer selves breaks down. There is an interpersonal bridge between our essential self (our inner world of feelings, body sensations, and spiritual insights) and the personality (that part of our psyche which interacts with the outer world). When this bridge is broken we are unable to access reliable information from the essential self. Basic needs such as nurturing, warmth, and connectedness with others go unmet and disregarded.

Anxiety - Distortion of our self image results. We experience ourselves as inadequate and unworthy of love. We fear that people around us will find out how insecure we are. In this psychic state of anxiety we work twice as hard, and try to be three times as nice, hoping that people will continue to like us and need us. All the while the

gap between the inner self and the outer self grows. With time it becomes even more impassable, because the communications have been disrupted and both systems are operating on inaccurate information.

Entrenchment - To give ourselves a feeling of security we adhere to our routines and our traditions whether they serve us or not. We do this primarily because we need a comfort zone of safety.

Too much change or change that is too rapid will unsettle our psychological equilibrium and cause us to feel even more anxious. Habits and routines, even the ones that are "unhealthy" or "dysfunctional," have a tremendous staying power because of **emotional inertia**. If you have ever tried to give up smoking cigarettes or eating too much chocolate, you will understand the extreme difficulty most people experience in breaking addictive patterns.

Inertia is the way we spare our internal circuitry. We can only process the amount of information that our inner computers can handle or risk "blowing a fuse." We are not "crazy" or at fault for being programmed to resist change. It is not a flaw in the inner workings of our computer. It's a way of maintaining integrity in a world full of changes. This is how we come to know our boundaries—by sensing them in a dynamic interchange with our environment and social interactions.

Boundaries

Boundaries are interfaces with the environment. Some are obvious, easy to see, like our skin marks the boundary of our physical body with the external world. Most boundaries can be changed: they can be made more permeable or more resistant, larger or smaller. We see that every time we gain or lose weight the skin stretches. They can be selectively permeable in response to the environment. They can heal. They can also be damaged beyond repair and lose their protectiveness and selectivity. Our boundaries fluctuate and change all the time because they are dynamic systems of protection and resistance.

Learning what our boundaries are, where we have choices, and how to implement these choices is an important part of caring for ourselves.

We all have limitations. They are an important part of our boundaries. Childhood is a process of testing boundaries (as parents are all too painfully aware). A successful childhood is one in which a child grows into a well-adjusted and flexible awareness of where his world ends and where the external world begins.

Many of us did not have totally successful childhoods, and there are gray areas in our understanding of boundaries. For some of us, it may be hard to say "no" when we do not want to do something. For others of us, it may be opportunities are missed because we have not acknowledged our strengths and talents. For all of us, finding and responding appropriately to the boundary interface will enrich our lives.

I have a healthy respect for my boundaries and limitations, yet I know they can be worked with and expanded. I do not have to accept they will always be there. I regard my limitations as signposts of where I can grow.

The Dynamics of Change

"Let ease show me where to go and tension show me where to grow."

—a self-affirming prayer

Life provides us with lessons all the time, so there are lots of opportunities for personal growth. The feelings which arise during these lessons give us the motivation to change the way we conduct our lives. If I may borrow from a famous scientist one of his formulas I can show you how this works:

$$E = mc^2$$

Energy = **m**otivation to **c**hange X **c**reativity

I am not sure if Einstein had this in mind when he was considering the mysteries of the universe, but these are physical dynamics which apply to any bundle of energy.

Most of the time we resist change. We like to use the same toothpaste, eat basically the same foods, and drive home the same way. We figure, "if it works for me, why change it?" But when something doesn't work we experience discomfort. That discomfort is emotional energy in its raw form (potential energy) and motivates us to try something new. The potential energy will not go anywhere until we make a decision, but once we make a decision, even if it is on a subconscious level, that change can take place.

Every time we decide to try something new, even if millions before us have made similar decisions, it is a creative act. It lays down new neural pathways, we add a new behavior to our repetoire of behaviors, and a ripple effect is generated in our field of influence that affects all contiguous areas of our lives and the lives of people in contact with us.

Creativity is powerful, isn't it?

Making a deliberate decision to expand be-yond our limitations is one of the most powerful decisions we can ever make.

I often find myself writing down my limitations as growth spots and forming a plan of action for them. Seeing them written down allows me to acknowledge the progress I've made at the end of the task, sets up a self-reward as I check them off my list, and allows me to learn more about myself if I don't change in the way I intended.

I use a four-step process to help me make the change.

1. **Define the task.** "Where do I need to focus?"
2. **What's the motive?** "What is the source and the amount of energy necessary to overcome the threshold of resistance?"
3. **Find the tools.** "What do I need to accomplish this task?"
4. **Read the directions.** "How do I get there?"

With any change, motivation is a key issue be-cause it represents **energy**. Many of us may think we are ready to make a change, but find it much too hard to overcome the threshold of resistance. Like any form of work in physics:

$$ERT \geq minT$$

The **E**nergy for the **R**equired **T**ransformation
must be equal to or greater than
the **min**imum needed to accomplish the **T**ask.

Imagine that you are an electron which is jumping up an orbit; there is a certain amount of energy the electron needs to absorb before it will move up. Even if you were to jump down an orbit—which ultimately leads to a release of energy—there is an initial amount needed to kick it out of orbit.

I think this explains the mysterious phenomenon of why it is hard to leave the house to go on vacation. I'm always behind schedule because it takes time and energy to wind things down and pack my suitcase. So what if I run a few orbits around the house? I'm checking to see if I turned off the stove, making a new message for the answering machine, and paying a last minute bill. It's all important. And once I'm done, I'm released emotionally. I can leap off into the vacation orbit.

Alien Robots and the Inner Child

When I was a child, I had nightmares about alien robots who would do things to me that took away my ability to move. They would inject me with a substance that took away my bones, or implant me with tapes that told me scary things, so that I was too paralyzed to move.

Through dream therapy I learned those alien robots were subconscious programs implanted by external events and people.

Those programs instructed me to act in addictive (robotic) patterns. They seemed to be a part of me, but they were not—hence the alien theme my dreams took.

Finding those alien programs, disabling them, and supplanting them with programs of choice has been my journey to freedom. The journey often took me through places in myself where I held a lot of fear. Overcoming the fear allowed me to step over the threshold of resistance into freedom of movement and making my own choices.

The Inner Child

If we are feeling spaced-out, anxious, or resistant, it is a sure sign that our inner self is angry or upset. The inner self is that part of our mind which is in charge of motivation and emotions. Like any child, or dog, or horse, it relies heavily on support, encouragement, and a sense of security to keep it going. If we ignore this part and force it to do things against its will, eventually it won't. The most dramatic example of the inner self working against us and defying our will is **self-sabotage.**

Self-sabotage seems mysterious, but only if we think our mind has one moving part. Ever since the time of Freud most psychologists have recognized the mind consisted of three parts: the subconscious, the conscious, and the superconscious mind.

The inner self is the portion of the mind that was programmed for us in childhood. How it views the world is colored by the quality of our childhood experiences. If we were brought up in a safe, supportive environment, the inner self sees the world as a safe and supportive place, and acts with confidence. A harsh and unstable childhood teaches the inner self that the world is an unsafe place. The inner self will have a lot of anxiety, lack self-esteem and confidence, and "overreact" to emotionally-charged situations.

An inner self which feels unsafe will sabotage any efforts to do scary things. For example, if we try to force the inner self to do something which it considers dangerous and stupid—like give a public speech—it will paralyze our throat with fear to keep us from making a fool of ourselves.

When we establish a rapport with our inner self, we build a bridge of communication from the inner to the outer self. We can prevent self-sabotage by communicating with it when we feel the inner self getting nervous. We can talk about its concerns, reassure it, and help it to get its needs met so we have its full cooperation in every venture we undertake.

The bonus to getting to know our inner self is the release of tremendous stores of power, self-awareness, confidence, and youthful energy. The inner self, when it feels cared for and understood, is wildly enthusiastic and helpful in every way. It is one of the best friends we will ever have.

One way we can help our inner self develop this state of enthusiastic cooperation is through "reparenting" ourselves.

The New Parent

It was the spring of 1973 and I was facing a tough exam in college. Anxiety and hard studying kept me awake all night. I knew I was not at my peak because I hadn't slept much, and the facts were not coherent. They spun around in my thoughts without making sense. I started to experience a panic.

A thought came to me—that I should act toward myself as the mother I always wanted. As I walked to my exam, I imagined that I was a warm and soft mother holding my baby self and reassuring myself that everything would be OK. I arrived at my exam in a much calmer state of mind, and passed the exam with a high score.

Years later, I am still doing this same meditation, as simple as it is, because it works. When I find myself judging myself, criticizing myself, or complaining about how other people are treating me, I go back to this vision. Often new inspirations, creative solutions and insights arise out of the release of anxiety because I think better when I am secure and happy. Instead of programming myself for anxiety and fear, I am programming myself for calm awareness and joyfulness.

Programmed for Fear

Most of us were brought up to follow a set of rules which we internalized at a very young age, sometimes in peculiar ways. We have rules about food, sex, other people's stuff, money, etc. so deeply ingrained in our perceptual framework that we don't even know they are there. Although it is an important part of the maturation process to learn to conform to the dictates of our society or suffer the loss of approval, love, and nurturing from significant people in our lives, there comes a point in our adult lives when we have to make our own decisions about how we conduct ourselves. Yet we are often thwarted in our decision-making by a substrata of "rules" which guide our unconscious choices.

When we were young, transgressions were punished and good behavior rewarded. We had to be trained in making discriminations, or we would have been much too feral to exist in society. You may have known people in which this kind of training was incomplete. Their behavior was uncomfortable and frightening. Even as a child, you knew you did not want to be like them because you could not trust them.

Parents, teachers, or their reasonable substitutes helped to form the way you would interact with the world. Most were well intentioned. But if they used threats or punishment, they were using fear to control your decisions. When fear rather than choice is used to shape behavior, the inner self suffers.

Traditional religions use much the same mechanism to shape the behavior and minds of their followers. Loss of love, nurturing, and approval are powerful motivators for "being good." However, fear of separation from God the Father (the parent made holy) peers and loved ones, supports a way of thought that divides us from our personal power.

Religion has done a lot for mankind. The power exerted by religion has been used for both constructive and destructive purposes. We are not condemning this coercion, only pointing out that it exists and examine the influence is has had on shaping our subconscious minds.

The members of any hierarchy have always feared the awesome individualistic psychic forces in the minds of its followers and saw the effectiveness of punishing individualism and rewarding self-denial in controlling those forces—ostensibly for the survival of the group, but just as often for the survival of the hierarchy.

For example, I was raised Protestant, and I am a recovering workaholic. The Protestant work ethic has us convinced that there's no gain without pain, sweat, and work. To do work we enjoy seems positively sinful. Healers especially suffer from this delusion, and many massage therapists, bodyworkers, and movement therapists are afraid to charge what they are worth, hence never seem to make enough to live on, even though they work very hard.

In order for us to move out of being controlled by external codes and to experience a healthy degree of personal freedom and compassion we have to let go of unfulfilling and destructive codes of behavior and develop a self-referent framework of values. This is not the same thing as narcissism. Let me explain...

False Gods and Glamour

Much of our modern culture is based on glamour and the promise of joy, security, and love. Acquisition of wealth, power, and objects of pleasure, personal appearance and social status take precedence over a sense of community and real connectedness with ourselves and others. We have a tendency to live on the surface of life—obsessed with our images and impressions of others. The status of the individual has been raised to godhood, so much so that a pervasive selfishness affects all levels of our lives, from our pop music to politics and corporate business decisions.

Many participants of the New Age are especially subject to this phenomenon, contrary to philosophy and to their utter frustration and bewilderment. The pressures of making a living in a consumer society drives us unmercifully, pulls us in several directions at once, and the cultural milieu and media play upon our fantasies and emotional strings as we try to stay afloat in a competitive marketplace.

Part of the problem is just the newness of the New Age—so many ideas, new technologies, and products have been generated by creative minds, that the grounding which comes from tradition and roots, the intimate connections with the familiar and old are not there.

The confusion and underlying angst is reflected by our frantic leisure time pursuits. Torn apart by diverse psychic forces, we force ourselves to self-improve by taking innumerable classes and work-shops, joining health clubs, dieting, consuming enormous quantities of vitamins and designer nutrients in the hopes of becoming smarter, sexier, and staying young forever.

Our restless search for self-improvement would suffice if being bright and beautiful was all we knew. But something haunts us, making us feel uneasy with ourselves. Deep inside of us reverberates a different set of values which undercuts and negates our efforts to be our fullest potential. Instead of becoming bright and beautiful we are haunted by the recurring thought that no matter what we do it's not good enough.

Even exercise becomes another form of self-abuse when we are encouraged to "go for the burn." Instead of having more choices we have more ways to feel guilty about ourselves. A sense of enjoyment and ease in the use of our bodies is sorely missing. We have been robbed of our inherent goodness because we have allowed a false and unnatural ethic to take the joy out of living.

The demands of our modern world are growing larger as our choices narrow. We have the semblance of freedom, but the modern person experiences a niggling suspicion that there is a loss of something they should be enjoying. There is a lot of context, but the content is missing in a lot of our lives.

The key words here are "content" and "context."

Context is the mental container in which we hold our experiences as we move through life. Context influences our perception of events and ultimately the way we experience reality. For example, there is a vast difference between my experience of writing a check to pay off a parking ticket and to buy a dress. Content is whether I experience a sense of annoyance or joy while writing the check.

I believe that practicing Self-Care enhances our ability to experience, sense, and record the content of our lives, and ultimately leads us to improve the context. It does this by developing in us an **internal frame of reference.** When we have a strong sense of who we are and where we are going with our lives, our self-esteem and sense of being right with ourselves and the world is high, our choices are freer and our motives purer. An internal frame of reference allows us the freedom to make our own choices to fill up the energetic reservoirs, strengthens the connection to the outer world, and gives us greater control over what influences us from the outside.

We no longer have to be under the influence of "alien robots."

Free Will and Choices

The best definition of freedom I have ever encountered is having the ability to choose. The ability is based upon, first of all, having the options, being able to perceive that there are options, and having the confidence to make a judicious decision about which one is the best. If we wish to cut through the dust and mold of our old traditions—and the confusion and illusions of the new ones—we have to make choices in our lives:

- We can choose a deeper connection with ourselves and with all the people we care about.
- We can choose to repair the interpersonal bridge and regain our essential selves.
- We can choose to take good care of ourselves and our personal environments.
- We can choose to feel supported, nurtured, and abundant.
- We can choose personal freedom over competitiveness.

These choices are not just a one-time decision, they are made up of many little decisions in a single day. The choice of making a phone call to someone in need of our services or staying home from work when we have a cold—these are the type of decisions which make up our life choices. If we have given thought to what our values are and stick to those values on a minute and intimate basis, an immense freedom from doubt and self-abasement ensues. Out of a place of choice, freedom, and personal power, we can work miracles.

Ending the War Within

Learning Self-Care is a process. It takes time to gain the ability to use our resources wisely. We have to work within the context of our every day lives, and in spite of our conflicting subconscious programs which we inherited from our parents, ancestors, peers, and the media.

Self-Care is a process of making peace.

Ask ourselves: is it time to end the war within? Can I negotiate peace among the different factions that drive me crazy when they criticize, demand, upbraid, and berate me? Will they learn how to cooperate and acknowledge how much they need each other?

As in all peace-making efforts, much of Self-Care is simply letting go of the past. There are old memories, ways of thinking, ways of seeing and reacting to events that we don't need anymore. It's important to continuously self-examine and deprogram dysfunctional ways of being. They may have worked at one time, but if they cause us harm, or just are in the way, taking up valuable space and consuming mental energy, then they are not appropriate to our current reality.

I know it's very easy to offer platitudes and aphorisms in a self-help book and sound like an expert. I'm not an expert, but the subject captivates and intrigues me. The more I study Self-Care, the more I care to know about the subject.

How do I take care of all the processes and details of keeping my body alive and healthy? I need a roof over my head, food on the table, I need to find, maintain and cultivate significant relationships, and somehow make enough time for a spiritual life and creative self-expression. That's a lot! How can I do it all and not go crazy or get burned out?

I know it's possible, because I've been able to do all these things, but it took time, thought, and commitment to work it out.

Life is a delicate interweaving of many threads, and the skill of the weaver is displayed in the intricacy of the pattern. I find my life challenging, demanding, and a lot of fun. So far I have woven a tapestry full of healing designs, rich colors, and intricate patterns. My life has not been all love and light—there are parts of the tapestry which are dark.

The grief and the shadows make the colors much more brilliant. I view my life like a work of art, and try to give it the same attention I would to weaving a beautiful tapestry. Every day's work matters to the whole piece so I try to live it the best I can.

Like weaving, Self-Care is an art and a discipline. The beginning of self-mastery is learning how to take life as it comes, gaining the ability to see what is really there, and working with real situations, instead of holding out for fantasies.

The **key** to Self-Care is to embrace life and to participate in the process of living to the fullest extent. The importance of participation to health is apparent if you have ever worked with the elderly. Most people gradually lose their will to live as they age.

It takes courage to face life and appreciate what is happening in the moment without indulging unduly in "what will happen if…" (fearing the future), or "if only…" (clinging to the past). We learn better and faster if we accept life as it is offered to us with all its bumps and scrapes, and all its experiences, offerings, and lessons.

Living a life well requires a great deal of sensitivity and intelligence and openness to our inner lives. It's important to remember:

None of us are handed a training manual on how to be a human being.

Many of us are making it up as we go along.

All of us are doing the best we can.

CHAPTER THREE

THE HEART PATH

Qualities of a Genuine Healer

Vitality
Responsiveness
Integrity
Genuine Caring
Accountability
Recognizes Value

Vitality

Healing is a transformative process, and like all transformative processes, healing needs a certain amount of energy to catalyze a change. Our vital energy levels need to be strong while we participate in a transformative process. When we are vital, we are more conscious, alert, less blocked by our personal dramas, and better protected against injury and disease. We are more likely to draw upon our place of creativity and higher resources.

To have high energy levels, we need to do more than drink a little wheat grass juice and eat bee pollen.

Vitality is the direct result of a balanced integration of the body/mind, emotions, and spirit. Each one must be in working order and flowing freely for us to be our most useful, productive, and effective as healers.

I know a lot of massage therapists and bodyworkers who complain of depression. We all get depressed once in a while, but when it happens a lot, something's wrong. A common cause of prolonged depression is low vitality levels. T'ai Chi masters spend their entire lifetimes learning to conserve, balance, cultivate and use chi, the vital life force. The traditions of these masters, if practiced religiously over a period of time, can bring our vitality levels up. We can keep them there by applying a few simple principles.

First of all, we need adequate rest and re-creation.

Second, we need to look at the ways we expend our energy. Are we making the most efficient use of our body? How about our time, emotional drives, and resources? One of the most influential teachers of my bodywork technique was a Kung Fu master who showed me that my fist strike was more effective if I stamped my foot and let the energy flow up through my center. Whole body movement is much more powerful than arm strength. The same applies to whole person movement.

Third, a daily practice of body-mind integration is essential to re-establishing our ties with our inner self. This may be T'ai Chi, yoga, meditation, or dance therapy. Anything that helps you acquire calming of the mind and body will accomplish this end.

Fourth, we need to remove the precious junk we've been hanging onto that is in the way of our growth. This means letting go of people who drain us, foods and substances which deplete our immune system, and disempowering thoughts from our subconscious minds.

How open are we to our life force? Look at the way you are holding your body. Feel your body alignment. Ask yourself these questions: *Is the head forward or back? Am I favoring one side over the other? Do I use the balls or the heels of my feet to stand? Am I moving with maximum efficiency?*

T'ai Chi focuses on alignment because it recognizes how important it is to the free flow of chi.

If you can imagine that the body is a series of conduit pipes stacked on top of each other, you can  visualize how easily the flow of chi can be cut off by the slightest misalignment in certain crucial spots. When my right shoulder droops, and my left sacro-iliac and right C-3 go out, that's a signal that I am being too serious and driven, and the soft, furry, fun-loving part of myself is being cut off. You may have a body signal that tells you when and where your life force is being cut off.

Body Signals to watch out for—stiff neck, tight shoulders, low back pain, heavy legs, tired feet, sore hands, "accidents," etc.

Responsiveness

One of the most healing and wonderful experiences is to feel nurtured on all levels of being, and to feel fully met in one's needs. The best bodyworker is not necessarily the one with the most training and technique, but the one which is present in the moment and responding to you as a whole person, not just as a body to be fixed. I'm sure all of us have had experiences with bodyworkers who did not have their minds or hearts engaged in the process. Do you remember how you felt afterwards?

One of the reasons I chose the word responsiveness to talk about instead of responsibility is because **responsiveness** is the ability to respond to each situation individually, without fixed ideas about the outcome. Responsibility often has been structured from a duty-bound ideal which can get in the way of true responsiveness. What is wrong with having responsibility, duty, and ideals? Nothing except **guilt** about not meeting unrealistic expectations, **self-accusation** and **blame** for everything that goes wrong, and an over-concern with what others think of us.

Feeling responsible for everything that goes wrong is a co-dependent behavior. Not all of you who are reading this book have this particular problem, but there's a significant number of co-dependents who are attracted to healing and will find this information useful.

Much of my life I have been co-dependent. I was the type of person who took on responsibility for much more than I wanted to or could handle because I felt duty-bound to do so. I was busy all the time and it felt like I was going somewhere but my friends had the kindness to point out to me I was spinning my wheels.

More recently I have been working from a self-caring place. I find I can respond to each individual's needs with integrity and still get my needs met as well. I don't self-sacrifice and I don't get overly weighted down with responsibility. Oops! Hardly ever...

Sometimes I catch myself falling back into old behavior patterns but I've learned not to beat on myself. Instead of abusing myself I have learned to laugh at myself and let it go. In order for an addictive behavior pattern to be released, we must first acknowledge that the behavior exists. Then we learn to love and accept ourselves just as we are, warts and all. This eliminates the shame and blame which the addiction was covering up.

Now that I focus more on being responsive than responsible, I find I take on only as much as I can bear, and I keep more promises. I also find myself less and less in desperate situations in which I need someone to come and save me from myself.

Integrity

Integrity is the finest quality a healer can have. From a place of integrity we act with the greatest intelligence and effectiveness. With integrity comes clarity, peace, and compassion.

Having integrity makes it easier to stay centered and balanced. Having integrity also allows us to be responsive to the needs of others without losing ourselves. From that place of center and balance, we are able to respond more sensitively to our environment.

What is integrity? Webster's University Dictionary defines it as: a state of being complete or whole; uprightness; virtue; honesty; soundness; unimpaired or unbroken state of anything.

The path to wholeness, uprightness, honesty, and virtue is a lifelong process. We are born with a special kind of integrity. We cry when we are hungry, sleep when we are tired, and laugh for the sheer joy of it. In this sense, we are born whole beings. But we lose our wholeness, our integrity, as we learn that not all our natural urges are desirable for those around us. We have to learn how to control our impulses and urges, but it separates us from our core being to do so. The ability to regain that integrity while interacting with our environment is developed as part of our maturational process.

Integrity is being sincere without being brutal, knowing our boundaries, energy levels and values, (but not having to announce them to everyone we meet.) It is living the way one chooses to live, instead of the way that was chosen for us. It is having purpose and direction in our lives—we know who we are and where we are going with our lives.

Integrity is **not** about building physical and psychic shields around ourselves. It's **not** about being strong all the time and it's **not** about holding one position indefatigably.

A common misconception about integrity is that it has a fixed quality to it. Integrity is not about having fixed ideals, that's fascism. True integrity has a fluid quality: it is the center of the being interacting sensitively with the influences surrounding it that gives a person integrity. People who desperately need to convince you of their goodness, worth, power, and righteousness are trapped in the **image** of having integrity.

Knowing ourselves (especially our strengths and our weaknesses) is a necessary part of integrity. Being able to love and accept ourselves exactly as we are allows us to love and accept others as they are without allowing them to harm or disempower us. Knowing, loving, and accepting ourselves enables us to face ourselves in our darkness, loneliness, and pain, as well as acknowledge and celebrate our power, goodness, and light.

By knowing ourselves we can make choices that

are in alignment with our inner wisdom, not the voices that bombard us. To provide ourselves with an immunity to the brainwashing and stimulus overwhelm around us, we need to develop our inner strength and wisdom. If we know ourselves well we can distinguish our thoughts from those that originate from outside influences, assess the reality of the situation, and respond powerfully, compassionately, and with full integrity.

Integrity helps to bring us out of desperation and to stay out of desperation. If we are filled with fear, lack, and frustration, we often make hasty decisions from a skewed perception. Our ability to see reality is distorted by our emotions. It is better to wait on making the decision, face the feelings which seem to block us, move through them to the other side, and make the decision when we feel clearer. We need integrity because we are not islands unto ourselves. We live in a **context** of physical, emotional, and subtle forces. We are completely immersed in a sea of impressions; our environment, media, religious upbringing, loved ones, and clients all color our thoughts. We are constantly interacting within this context, **co-creating** a reality with the other actors in our environment. Only by coming from a place of integrity can we maximize our ability to create the reality we want. This is personal power.

Integrity doesn't happen in a vacuum. It happens under stress, in extreme situations, and under pressure. It's easy to **seem** to have integrity when there are no demands upon us, but the real test of integrity is under duress. Stressful situations bring out the best and worst in people.

As healers we well know how many disease states are stress-related. Stress drains our energy, and makes it harder to fight off diseases, and to clean out autotoxins. Yet paradoxically, stress can also have an innervating, rejuvenating effect. If we can learn how to move harmoniously with our internal and external flows, we won't get drained in extreme circumstances. In fact, those very circumstances can begin to lend impetus to our journey by using the emotional energy that they arouse in us.

A bodysurfer once described to me, quite elegantly, the way this energy can be used:

When I'm standing on the beach I can see the energy lines in the waves and where the maximum force is in the wave. That's the part of the wave, if you know what you're doing, where you can ride the longest. I get as close as I can to that point. When I'm ready, I get low down in the wave until I'm actually standing on the node of energy. That's what I ride into the beach as if I had been shot out of a cannon. (Conversation with Dan Riley, world champion bodysurfer.)

If we can learn to master the flows, we can get there faster and with more ease.

A major cause of stress is not knowing what to do. In order to best be able to aid others it helps us to have **direction** and **purpose** in our lives. If we know where we're going and what we are doing to get there, that gives our emotional energy a **channel** in which to flow.

If we have some of the important questions about life answered it makes it easier to know what to do in any given situation. Some of the important questions are:

Who are we?
What we are doing with our lives?

Where we are going?

What would we like to accomplish?

There are no right or wrong answers to these questions. Simply asking them lends us insight into ourselves, our desires, and our lifepath.

If you haven't asked yourself these questions lately, it might be useful to sit down and write the answers to these questions and post them somewhere where you'll see them a lot. I have found seeing them written down helps me keep on purpose and allows me to acknowledge the progress that I've made. From a place of self-direction and harmonious interaction the so-called "negative" emotions spur me on to greater changes and help me to clarify what I want.

Genuine Caring

We are born with an incredible power: the ability to create our own reality. However, this power is not given to us at birth; it is a skill that must be mastered as we grow into our lives. It is developed through conscious intent, experience and thoughtfulness, and through the exercise of free will, personal authority, and power. **Genuine caring cannot exist unless it is supported by our personal power.** It enables us to give in ways that not only empower us, but others. It is having power **with** others instead of having power **over** others.

Creating the reality we want at the expense of others is not desirable. At some point in your life that form of power will create jealousy, dissension, and misgivings for you. Some people live their life as if they had no tomorrow. The problem is that there is a tomorrow and we are responsible for creating it.

Would it not be better to create more supportive and nurturing situations?

As our personal power increases, the ability to influence others also increases. We must not confuse personal power with the ability to control events and people; it is not the same kind of power. **Personal power** is the ability to create more satisfying realities. It is important to know when it is beneficial and useful to exercise the power to influence others and when it is not. We can avoid the traps of having great power if we remember our humanness with love and affection. It keeps us humble.

I don't know how many times I've had clients say, "You healed me!" and I have to say to them "I was here helping, but you healed yourself." And I have to do that for myself. I have a lot of self-esteem about the abilities, skills, and insights I use, but if my personality slips into the big ego place, I lose integrity and get a painful lesson in humility.

We are guides on the path for our clients, not gods. The power to heal flows through us, but we don't own it. We co-create it with our clients.

> *We thought we were gods,*
> *And we were.*
> *But in the midst of our earth-bound ways*
> *We forget what we chose to let go of*
> *And pretend we are not what we are.*
> *We forget that*
> *We chose to lose something old,*
> *In order to gain something new.*
>
> —Mary Jane Evans, 1976

Accountability

Along with integrity and genuine caring, a self-caring healer possesses accountability. The Old French verb *'acompter'* from which this term arises means to reckon, to answer, to consider, to regard.

To be accountable we must have confidence in ourselves and know our abilities. We can **reckon** on what we can **give** because we know what we **have.** People can count on us to deliver what we say we will provide. People can count on us to be at a place at the time we agreed upon. People can count on us because we can count on ourselves to deliver what we promise.

Accountability is a combination of integrity (knowing ourselves and what our resources are at any given time), and good communication. We may have a lot of integrity, but if we can't communicate what we can give to others in a way that they can get it, they'll never know it.

With accountability we know what we have and we can tell others what we can do for them. If people ask us what our work is like, we can **answer** them clearly and succinctly because we know what our work can do for them. Like integrity, accountability does not have to be forced or based on inflexible rules. We simply **consider** others in our decisions. We choose to keep an appointment not because we'd feel so guilty if we didn't, but because we are accountable. If we are ill we might choose to postpone the appointment, but we do so with enough advance notice so that a person can adjust their schedule. If we can't make it on time we do our best to contact the person or persons involved. If we have problems with being late for appointments we learn to leave the house earlier. Why? Because we are accountable.

Accountability is valuing others because we value ourselves. We **regard** them as equally valuable human beings due the same kind of respect we would want for ourselves.

Being accountable engenders trust, and when people trust you it's easier to establish rapport and ultimately be in a healing relationship.

Recognizing Value

My clients **are** my business. Without my clients I would not be a bodyworker or have a practice. My clients are very valuable to me, not just because they give me money, but because I enjoy them. We have a relationship in which we exchange one good thing for another.

I came upon a little piece called "What is a Customer?" that describes this relationship perfectly. It was part of a sales training I took. It's anonymous, but whoever wrote it, I thank them here. It's a beautiful piece about value.

I've substituted the word "client" for customer and paraphrased some parts, but for me it's one of the most useful things ever written about an important principle of business, the mutually beneficial exchange. This is the piece:

A client is the most important person in our business. A client is not dependent on us. We are dependent on them. A client is not an interruption of our work day, they are the purpose of it. A client does us a favor when they call. A client is an integral part of our business—not just a stranger. A client is not just money in the bank. They are human beings with feelings and deserve to be treated with respect. A client is a person who comes to us with their needs and wants. It is our job to fill those we can and do our best to direct them to where they can fill those we can't. Clients are the lifeblood of this and every business. Without them we would have no business. And we will never forget this simple little fact.

Our clients have value. They have a right to ask for their wants and needs to be met, and if we can serve them, we do so with joy.

In our interactions with our clients there might be situations which test this ideal. For example, a client might always show up late, then want to have a full session, even though there are clients behind him or her. If we value ourselves and our time, and that of all our clients, we can explain to the late client what our late policy is. And we do it without blame or shame. For example, at the chiropractic clinic where I once worked as a massage therapist, we told our clients this:

Our sessions are scheduled for one hour. So many minutes are allotted for communicating special needs, so many minutes for undressing, and so many minutes are actually hands-on time. To serve you best and to maximize our time together, it would be better if we kept our agreed upon time. I understand there are extenuating circumstances, but I have clients after you that I have to serve as well as you and to be fair to everyone, I can't run overtime. I have set this time aside for both of us to work together and when we start at the appropriate time there should be enough time to accomplish everything we need to accomplish.

You may not have someone coming in the next hour, but it would behoove you to tell your client what your policy is even if you don't have someone coming after them, because theoretically someday you will. If you have established guidelines beforehand it will make sticking to them easier when you really need to.

There's another aspect to value. We want to get the most out of life and sometimes being too busy interferes with our ability to take life in, let alone enjoy it. We need to be jealous of our time, and make sure that we are doing what we want as much as possible. Joseph Campbell said it well when he instructed us to "follow our bliss." It is up to us to listen to our hearts, bodies, and our deepest truth to know what bliss is.

Follow Your Bliss

CHAPTER FOUR

THE SELF-CARING HEALER

Qualities of a Self-Caring Healer:

Balances giving with receiving
Takes time out for re-creation
Listens to heart
Listens to body
Listens to mind
Listens to inner child

Giving and Receiving

In a mutually beneficial exchange, both parties get something from the exchange. Giving and receiving are well-balanced. The result is everyone ends up with more of what they needed or wanted than they had before the exchange. Mutually beneficial exchange is a good example of the old adage: the sum of the whole is greater than its parts.

Mutually beneficial exchange is the **ideal.** Sometimes **reality** is different, and the free flow of exchange gets fouled up. We healers are natural givers, but not all of us are natural receivers.

Many of us grew up in families where we learned to deny our needs for the sake of the family.

In the dysfunctional family environment, we learn reticence and self-restraint, not as virtues, but as a form of survival. Certain types of communication are repressed. Asking for what we needed and wanted brought attention to us and often led to disappointment, shame, verbal and/or physical punishment.

When communication is discouraged, our emotional stuff gets wrapped up in pretty little packages and we take turns throwing it at each other. Sometimes we don't take turns and we don't bother to put it in pretty packages. Things get ugly. Nobody in the family is allowed to talk about this outside the family. We try to hide what we're really doing from the rest of the world. The conversation forms around the family secret, without our ever having to mention "it," but the absence in the words we speak casts a big shadow.

In the dysfunctional family we learn to tolerate the family's little lies and to cover up our mistakes. We were told God, Santa Claus, or Daddy would punish us as soon as they found out what we did (or did not do.) The less "they" know the better off we are. We learned that by not having any needs we could get by with what we had and minimize the pain of bad things happening to us.

To break free of this conditioning we need to regain the ability to sense what our needs are and get them met in appropriate ways.

For many of us who grew up in dysfunctional families, self-esteem is a problem. Part of our healing is growing away from the unhealthy family milieu, and establishing who we really are. Many people recover from their dysfunctional childhoods and grow strong in their sense of self-esteem. **No matter how bad our childhood was, as an adult we have the power to change.**

I've done a lot of work with raising my self-esteem. One of the most effective techniques I've used is to record a tape, in my own voice, of affirmative declarative emphatic statements I wanted to believe about myself.

Script for Audio Tape

I am a Self-Caring Healer. I know the universe is going to give me everything I need. I recognize that I have to put concentration and effort into getting my needs met. I have all the resources I need to take care of myself now.

I know that for every step I take in the direction of getting my needs met, the universe takes ten steps to help me.

I came into this world with a unique gift, and that gift will help me get my needs met. No one has this gift in the same way I do. This gift was designed for me, by me, with me. I offer this gift to humanity. I intend to use it wisely, and to get it to the right people.

The universe is more than willing to help me. In fact, in my more resplendent moments, I often get the feeling of it falling over itself trying to help me. There are ways in which I can help it help me: by being peaceful, thankful, and staying committed.

If I am feeling unappreciated in my present relationships, I can change that feeling by expressing appreciation in as many places and ways as I can.

If I am still not getting the appreciation I need and want, I am asking the wrong people to appreciate me. I need to search for people who will appreciate me for the wonderful person that I am.

If I am discontent because no one seems to want my gift, instead of disposing of the gift, I may only need to change the way I present it to bring me the success I long for.

What I have to offer is of great value. And there are people waiting for me, who are willing to appreciate me, and who want what I have to offer.

This technique was even more effective when I recorded three versions of the same script with the different persons: "I, Maja Evans, am a Self-Caring Healer." "Maja, she is...," "Maja, you are..." I used it a lot: every time I felt low, to go to sleep, before my work day, in the car...

Re-creation

The basic forms of self-renewal are rest, play, music, dance, storytelling, time alone, time in nature, time in bed, and a good massage.

I cannot stress the importance of recreation enough. For the Self-Caring Healer it is a must. We have a lot to give the world as healers, but we must take care of ourselves in the process. How do we know when to stop giving so that we can receive? When is it appropriate to withdraw from our lives so that we can renew our strength? Where can we recharge our batteries? The answer is simply "Listen to your body."

When I am driven and obsessive it is a signal that I am getting my adrenals overexcited and I need to take some time out. When I am over that edge my legs get very tired and heavy. In the past I wouldn't stop to rest because I heard this voice in my head saying, "I've got to get this done." I could feel myself getting irritable, and like a child who is hyper and cranky, I would not go to sleep until I "crashed." Sometimes when I am in this state, I literally crash into things: like furniture, sliding glass doors, or crash up against another equally irritable person. This takes the fun out of life.

It's hard to get a handle on it because it's biochemical—my adrenals think we're under attack, but it's only stress. Because I know I am this way, I have had to develop a lot of stress management techniques to use when I get in this state. I'm gradually training myself to stop and go lie down when I hear that voice, feel my lower back tighten up, or I start crashing into things.

I find getting a massage is helpful for bringing me back into my body. I know how hard it is for some of us to give ourselves permission to do that because resistance keeps us wanting to go on. I have to go through my resistance to slowing down and letting go. Allowing myself to be nurtured brings up childhood issues about touch and control. I go through all of these emotions and thoughts, before I even get on the table. I know massage will switch me from my angry, fearful, anxious, driven personality to my soft, fun loving, and creative personality. The chemical change is from an excess of adrenaline and noradrenaline, the neurotransmitters of the fight or flight syndrome to more endorphins, the relaxation-healing neurotransmitters.

We need to get back what we give out so that we do not exhaust our resources. As body therapy professionals we are responsible for our health and well-being, not for our client's sake, but for our own.

The reason why healing touch is so effective is that it affects the non-verbal parts of our nervous systems, giving this affirmative message to our inner world—"you are loved."

Listening to Our Hearts

Listen to our hearts—how many times have we told ourselves to do that? Then we turn around and do what we think we should be doing, not what we want?

It's a challenge to sort all the other voices inside our hearts. Finding the "still small" voice that is our own is difficult enough, but having the courage to follow it is much harder.

First we have to weed through the voices of our authority figures—parents, teachers, principals, New Age gurus, and lovers. Then we have to wade through the gossip and superstitions of our siblings, peers, and friends. Finally we have to turn off the mental commercials. All the voices that result from our culture's media bombardment, especially the voices which promise a false ease and pleasure (if we just do this thing or have that widget) which cheat us out of enjoying the moment. We have to weed out all these voices to discover what is really going on with us.

How many times have we made a promise to do something but instantly regretted it? Then we find our stomach is getting tight and our jaws clamp? This is a sure sign that we have lost touch with ourselves, with that special part that warns us of difficulty or approaching danger. The thing we promised to do may even be a pleasurable activity, but we don't have the time or we're already overextended. It's just not going to work for us and we know it in our gut.

We may not see the alternatives: saying no, admitting we're overextended, or changing our priorities so that our needs are taken care of also.

Ignoring the tight stomach will just give us indigestion, and tight jaws. However, if we allow ourselves to acknowledge the stress reaction, make an intelligent choice, and act on it, this will keep our relationships clean.

One of the best ways to know our hearts is to observe how our body responds to specific thoughts. Body reactions tell us when we are excited and happy, or if we are threatened and ready to strike.

While we are watching our body react to specific thoughts, it is a good time to be detached from our judgemental selves. We should regard our body's wisdom to see what is really there. The moment we start to criticize ourselves for having a feeling, we cut ourselves off from feeling it.

Another way to tell what is happening with our hearts is to watch our lives because they reflect our thoughts. By observing our external situation, we can gain insight about our internal environment.

The world often mirrors our thoughts back to us; if we are angry inside, we often find ourselves surrounded with angry people. The world is an imperfect mirror; we do not need to assume we created everything in our lives, all the good and all the bad. If we let go of blaming ourselves and criticizing others, then we can begin to see reality for what it is.

Our only task is to clean the mirror.
— Buddhist saying

For many of us when we listen to our hearts we sometimes hear just confusion and pain. When this happens to me, I just say to myself, "Well, that's what's in there. So what? I choose to be with what is real for me."

When I affirm my desire to be with my emotions instead of hiding from them, listening to my heart is easier.

It is natural to run away from the pain. Pain is

uncomfortable. We **overcompensate** and **under-mine** to escape the pain. We overcompensate by speeding up activity, becoming more extroverted, or by taking stimulants. We undermine by resisting, withdrawing, and "tuning out". All of this just to get out of the feeling of painful.

It is a great temptation to be hard on ourself when we act out our compulsions. So what? It happens all the time. Everybody has their little piece of imperfection. We want to be there for the people we love in our lives, be the perfect mother or father, lover, healer, and person, but it's hard when the feelings overwhelm us. Life doesn't work on the principles of perfection. It works on the principles of evolution and growth, which involves a degree of error programmed into the system.

Your best is all you can do. If you think you can do better and you don't, you still did your best. Do it better at your next opportunity. Doing better comes naturally if we love ourselves for who we truly are, acknowledge our imperfections and our progress.

The journey back to my heart happens every day, sometimes several times a day. Wisdom has taught me to lead myself back to my heart gently. I know how much it helps to relax, breathe, and take some time to be alone.

Sacred time is possibly the most powerful way in which we can heal ourselves. A retreat from our mundane reality with all its details and demands is absolutely necessary part of any self-care program. It can be a walk in the woods, a vacation, a time spent with good friends. The definition of sacred is that which is outside of the profane i.e., our ordinary or "real" lives. It is a time and space outside of ordinary time and space, for putting aside all of our cares, worries, and responsibilities in order that we may spiritually renew ourselves. The ancients understood this. We can reclaim it.

Solitude is especially important for caregivers. It gives us the necessary space to clear ourselves after helping others clear themselves.

We **deserve** this time to ourselves, to meditate, to pamper ourselves, to introspect, to re-establish our values.

As healers, much of our life is spent dealing with other human beings on levels of fear, anger, and longing. We gain a lot of growth from interacting with each other, indeed it is hard to grow without it, but in solitude we realize the fruit of these human interactions.

Aloneness is a very full and beautiful feeling. Quite often our relationships fill in our loneliness, but exclude our chance to know ourselves better. Those of us who are in a relationship, or work with people day in and day out, are going to need time just for ourselves.

Listening to Our Bodies

The human body is like a very expensive, finely tuned automobile. Our bodies are constantly talking to us—they whisper, shout, sputter, and purr. If we give our bodies the "Rolls Royce" treatment, they return the favor. But if we give our bodies the wrong fuel, race the engine, and forget the lubrication, then we get poor performance. We get sick, tired, we catch colds easily, our digestion and moods get off balance.

When this happens we lose touch with ourselves and our effectiveness as healers.

The body is the vehicle. The spirit is the driver. We use our body to move about and interact in the world of physical matter. Without it, our spirits could not grow or evolve in this plane. Infinitely precious, and exquisitely beautiful, our bodies are irreplaceable. They deserve the very best treatment we can give them.

A hangover from our spiritual training is the concept that this world is illusion and our bodies are full of desires, lusts, and drives that are better off ignored, suppressed and denied. Self-control does not come from self-denial—only spiritual materialism, psychological damage to the low self, and a build-up of psychic guilt over food, sex, and other necessary functions of life.

This world is real, our bodies are real, and the need for the spirit to grow and evolve in the body machine is very real. Instead of becoming more "spiritual," and transcending our "gross" desires, we would be better off learning how to align our spirits with our minds and bodies, so that our growth is harmonious, balanced, and healthy.

Balancing the mind with the body is more than a wish, an affirmation, or a good intention. It is a commitment to taking care of ourselves on a daily basis. So what if we have to eat health food, exercise appropriately, and take time out to renew ourselves? It can be a lot of fun if we do it with the two sisters, Zest and Zeal.

The Two Sisters, Zest and Zeal

When we listen to our bodies, how do we know what they are saying? Simply by being sensitive to them. If you have a close long-term relationship with a cat, dog, a child, you learn to read its signals for food, attention, pain, and boredom. You get sensitive to its needs through rapport.

To gain rapport with anything you have to clear away all your ideas and emotional stuff about this animal, child, body, or person. Then you have to look and listen to what s/he/it is saying, not what you think s/he/it is saying. I liken this to learning how to walk with a dog: lead it firmly but gently. To drag it along unwillingly on a tight leash, or let it run loose all over the place, is not loving if it causes harm and frustration to the dog and you.

There is a process in the work I do called "Gentling." I explore the boundaries of the person I am working on to find out where I can take them without having to force my way in. I look for the ways the body wants to go, and where it is willing to let me in. This builds a lot of trust between the therapist and client. The process takes more concentration, time and sensitivity than the deep tissue work I used to do, but the results are more permanent.

"Gentling" can be applied to every aspect of our lives, from dietary change to mental house cleaning. There is no need to be harsh with ourselves, only persistent, definitive, and active.

Listening to Our Minds

We are constantly involved in the process of bringing to consciousness unconscious desires, memories and habits that a part of us would rather not look at. If we compare our minds to gardens, self-destructive thoughts and impulses are like weeds. As any good gardener knows, we need to trace weeds to their roots before we can get rid of them, not trim the leaves.

Suppose you smoke cigarettes and want to quit. You go to a hypnotherapist, throw away your cigarettes, and quit smoking. Then you gain twenty pounds because you can't stop eating ice cream.

It doesn't help you to get rid of a habit unless you get rid of the reason why you have that habit in the first place.

What's the root of *this* problem? It might be a reluctance to breathe, or a need to be nurtured, or a fear of being loved. The answer is inside you and as you come to consciousness, as you grow, the answer will come to light naturally. Just listen to your mind.

Unless you do a lot of drugs, are brain dead, or have many lifetimes of meditation behind you, your mind will talk constantly. It's like a **radio**. The internal voices comment on everything that goes on around you, sorts, categorizes, imagines all kinds of possibilities, and plays you snatches of music.

It's the spaces I listen to, the stuff in between the constant chatter. What is the chatter trying to cover up? What is my mind trying to tell me? If I breathe and relax for a moment, what image will pop into my head? The answer comes in the spaces and the pauses.

I also gather information about my internal state by the **song** my mind is currently playing. Rock n' roll, Walt Disney songs, torch songs all have a theme and a meaning. "Please release me, let me go..." is a song I used to sing a lot.

Sometimes I have voices which tell me to do things I know I don't want to do. I know those are "not-self" voices, sort of like viruses in the computer.

They are revealing of my inner state because they signal low energy or self-esteem problems.

I know when I can get my mind quiet, I am living entirely in present time. Moments of silence are like pearls. If I string enough of them together, I'll have something I value—peace.

Listening to the Inner Child

Inside each of us is a sweet, lovable, enthusiastic, and playful person who wants to serve us in every way it can. Part of the way it wants to serve us is to show us the true value of things. Like all children, the inner child loves hugs, smiles, and a little acknowledgment for a job well done.

The inner child is involved in the functions of motivation, moods, and memory. It is a valuable and delicate part of our mind and needs a lot of support, encouragement, and nurturing in order to work properly. Too often we ignore this part, verbally abuse it, or downplay its importance, and that makes it resistant, recalcitrant, and reticent. It's important to acknowledge that it is always doing the best it can, so we need to feed it the right kind of information about ourselves and give it lots of strokes for a job well done.

A well-cared-for inner child is sweet, loving, eager to participate and learn. Whenever we feel good, it's because our inner child is feeling safe, happy, and taken care of. There's nothing more important than to engage and nurture the little child inside by keeping life fun. Through the activity of play we express our inner child, exercise (and exorcise) our bodies and minds, learn new things, explore new territories, let go of old problems, and see the comedy of life.

The inner child hates being bored, so a little excitement and adventure will go a long way. One of my favorite jokes is to say: "Don't Work, Be Happy! Let's Play." (a slight variation on a Newageism). I'm a confirmed playaholic, and there's no recovery in my future. I have a lot of fun with my inner child. Although my work may look like work on the outside; to me it's a high form of play.

In addition to doing bodywork, I've spent a lot of time with children as a resident intern, storyteller and clown. These experiences have taught me the importance at laughing at myself with love in my heart like the children do. If we can be more childlike (and less childish), our lives will be filled with more love and laughter, and fun.

One of the things that really helped me become more attuned to my inner child was the frequent use of a Self-acceptance Script that was part of a Personal Marketing workshop. I have it hanging in my bathroom so I read it while I'm brushing my teeth. I try to do this on a daily basis, and I made a tape of the script which I play to myself when I find myself feeling down. It has a magical effect on my psyche. I become very peaceful and open to life's experiences when I listen to this tape.

The script is designed to acknowledge, support, and encourage your subconscious mind, especially that part which is referred to as the "Inner Child."

The script can be found in the book, Rapid Personal Growth by Stanley E. Russell, Ph.D., which can be ordered by calling or writing him at:

Russell Dynamics, Inc.
P.O. Box 101
Mill Valley, CA 94942
(415)383-0451

CHAPTER FIVE

DEVELOPING THE SELF-CARE HABIT

The Health Regime

In building a successful practice, the demands of our business become all-consuming, and our busy schedules tax our body's capabilities to withstand stress. Setting aside a special time every day to pay attention to the body/mind is absolutely essential if we want to stay healthy. Many of us already have good habits: the habit of eating well, a regular exercise program and a meditation period every day, yet we feel we are not doing enough. If this describes the way you feel, then you may enjoy reading this chapter, because it talks about the power of self-acknowledgment in creating health.

For those of you who are still struggling with maintaining a regular health regime, this chapter will support you in developing an individualized self-care program that will ensure the high vitality and mental alertness needed for our profession.

Maintaining a health regime when we are under stress is about the hardest thing we'll ever have to do and this is the time we need it most. We will know that we've got the Self-Care habit when we start doing more for our health regime when we get under stress than when we do when we're not under stress.

Stress is not such a bad thing when we know how to use it wisely. We have a number of stress indicators which protect us when we are under too much stress—much like your house has circuit breakers that go off when too much juice is running through a wire.

I call these stress indicators "my alarm systems." When the bells go off, I go looking for the stress and its cause, and then look for ways to eliminate or reduce the stress. For me, my stress indicators are my bladder, my back, my skin, and my right arm. On an emotional level, feeling short, irritable, and wanting to be alone are alarms telling me it's time to cool down. On a mental level, if I get too manic, talk too fast, or space out, I know I'd better stop the world and get off long enough to do a deep relaxation.

As we develop more body awareness, we can catch these stress indicators before they get to the disease state and save ourselves a lot of pain and suffering. Being sensitive to our bodies needs' is a crucial part of our health regimes, as important as having sound minds and bodies. The following sections on meditation, movement, breath, massage and diet are based on my personal experience with developing a self-care program. You may have other things that work for you, which is good. Do what works for you. The best self-care program you can devise is based on your individual needs, not some prescription out of a book.

The Program

The first step in the self-care program is simply to pat ourselves on the back for everything we do that is good for ourselves. Make a list of all the good things you do. You'll be surprised to see how much is really there.

Acknowledging the good that we do for ourselves is very important to creating motivational foundation for self-care. Our inner selves need encouragement and appreciation. When we stroke ourselves for our goodness, we enroll our inner child in doing even more good things for our body/minds. Like any child, the inner child responds well to praise. Punishment, criticism, judgement, and abuse only makes a child resistant and fearful.

Then list all the things you would like to change, add, or subtract from your habits, obsessions, and addictions, then prioritize them for how easy each one would be to accomplish. Take the easiest one on the list and do that one this week, the next easiest one next week, and so on. If you start with the easiest one, you're very likely to experience success in accomplishing your goal. This encourages the inner child to continue progress.

Our inner selves love to succeed, and they will put their full effort behind anything they think they can do. However the inner child can be easily set back and discouraged if the expectations are too high for what they think they can do. Choose reasonable goals.

After you have done this for several weeks, go back to your list to note how much progress you've made with your self-care program. Write it down. This step is very important because it imprints on the mind that the goal has been accomplished. It will complete the thought, and you will be able to move on to the next one.

We might start to notice that our goals change over time and we may not want the same things for ourselves that we wanted last year, or even last month. It's OK to change our minds if something is not working for us. Let's not put ourselves down or frustrate ourselves with fixed ideas of "the way it's supposed to be." Sometimes it's better just to accept the fat or the wrinkles, because the stress of trying to get rid of them is causing more fat and wrinkles. The more we love ourselves, the healthier and more attractive we will be, and the quicker we can effect desirable changes in our lives.

In summary—it's important to see our progress and pat ourselves on the back frequently for our successes. This will lead to more success.

Meditation

Slowing down helps us develop rapport with our bodies. Our culture is a driven culture in more ways than one. The automobile and airplane have speeded up our lives. The TV and cinema have increased the amount of information we take in.

Slowing down enables us to bring our awareness into our bodies and out of our heads. For example, it's the middle of the afternoon and you're tired. You may think your body wants a cup of coffee, but it really needs is a few deep breaths and a mental break. If you can get into the habit of taking a few deep breaths, you can eventually bring your wants and needs in harmony.

The best way to slow down is meditation. Stopping the body helps to still the mind. A calm mind sends neurohormonal signals to every cell in your body saying, "It's safe now, let's rest and rejuvenate." The muscles relax, the immune system starts to clean out the debris, and the hormones associated with comfort and pleasure are released. A reinforcing circle is set up, your body gets used to being relaxed, secure, and grounded.

The more you meditate, the greater the benefits. A regular practice enables you to go very deep with your body, especially if your meditation system focuses on body and breath.

Some meditative forms have a tendency to get you out of your body, they are very useful for spiritual development, but not for developing body awareness. The meditative forms that focus on breath (ex. Zen) and body awareness (ex. walking meditation) are the most useful in this case.

Slowing down in our everyday life helps us gain greater body awareness. When we rush from here to there, push ourselves to get the job done on time, or if we have a million things to do in a day, it is hard to stay in our bodies. Slowing down our lives may mean cutting out a few things, but then we can take in more and enjoy it more. The benefits of relaxing far exceed the strokes we get for being "superpeople".

Once you get your awareness in your body in your everyday life (not just when you are working, meditating, or in session), then you can start paying attention to how you move through your day. Do you tense your lower back while you brush your teeth? How do you pick up heavy objects? Do you tighten your right anterior tibial while driving? Developing this kind of awareness expands your understanding of the body. This extra dimension of "self" consciousness enhances our work with other people.

Movement

Moving our bodies keeps them in a fluid state. Tightening, stiffening, overtaxing parts of our bodies freezes those parts. Energy flow and circulation get blocked. We start to lose mobility.

Here's a little trick for when you encounter stiffness in your body—just move it. Movement brings in fresh blood, unlocks contracted muscle tissue, and gets rid of toxic waste.

T'ai Chi Ch'uan and Yoga are movement forms which help develop body awareness. They focus on appropriate placement of your body in space and building strength, flexibility, and the flow of chi (vital energy).

If you are not in excellent condition, you may find benefit in learning one of these forms before you attempt strenuous exercise, such as Aikido, aerobics, and running. They are deeply strengthening form of exercise because of their emphasis on internal exercise as well as external exercise. They play an important role in general health-building because, in addition to building cardiovascular and muscular endurance, they strengthen the joints, bones, and internal organs.

Sports injuries are much less likely to happen with these forms because you learn how to move in alignment. Many injuries happen from moving out of alignment. The chronic stress caused by misalignment leads to weakness in that joint. Seemingly insignificant movements can result in a painful acute injury. Aerobics, weight training, and running have great benefits, but they also have great potential for injury if not done with sensitivity and care for the body.

Yoga and T'ai Chi are especially good for alignment and breath awareness. Once you have alignment and breath awareness, you might want to try a more strenuous form of exercise. I like Aikido because I love the playfulness it brings out in me. Aikido has an added advantage in that it teaches the body to fall down and to get up from the fall, and to use the attacker's energy for your self-defense. It is very good for developing a three-dimensional awareness of your body movement.

Aikido has other applications beside self-defense, it can be a life-style. In Aikido philosophy there are no enemies, only potential friends who attack because they are in a state of temporary ignorance. The point of Aikido, to defuse or immobilize the attacker so you can reason with him, can be a useful life philosophy, as well as a physical self-defense system.

Aikido philosophy can also be applied to our attitudes about ourselves. Most of us feel in a state of war with ourselves and exercise with a vengeance. If we can exercise with a sense of fluidity and playfulness, we will see our body as a friend and be more respectful toward it.

Bodywork systems which focus on movement education can help your alignment, breath patterns, and grounding. Feldenkrais, Alexander, Hellerwork, and Aston Patterning are some of the better known systems.

Breath

Breath awareness in and out of the session is absolutely essential for bodyworkers. The breath is an incredibly sensitive barometer of emotional state. Holding the breath is a sign of stress, intense concentration, fear, anger, sadness, or fatigue.

Most of us have developed shallow breath patterns because of unreleased stress responses. Holding the breath helps you concentrate on an immediate situation; it is part of the stress response. It is also useful for shutting off feelings when expressing them would not be appropriate.

However, when the immediate situation is over,

the emotional stress and breath should be completely released, and often are not. Freeing the breath mobilizes thought, emotion, and action. It is a very powerful tool for getting "unstuck" in life.

We can utilize spare moments as a meditation on the breath. In the bank line, waiting for your spouse, in the midst of a traffic jam, situations that usually are stressful take on a new dimension. They become opportunities for greater relaxation and ease.

Developing a deep soft full breath pattern can be a lifetime goal of concentrated fun, a way of developing effortlessness in our activity.

Watching a baby sleep is a good meditation on breath. Infants breathe naturally when relaxed, their abdomen and chest rise and fall rhythmically, effortlessly.

If your bodywork or meditation system already has a method of focusing on breath, you have a head start. See if you can apply the principles to all aspects of your life. Especially focus on the times when you are most likely to hold your breath. Whenever you:

1. Make an effort,
2. Defend yourself in an argument,
3. Deal with unpleasant sensations (diapers),
4. Use the abdominals (shoveling snow).

There are certain chemical substances which affect the free flow of breath on a subconscious level, so when you take in those substances you may want to monitor your breathing for several hours following the exposure.

In particular, air pollution, cigarette smoke, alcohol, marijuana, and stimulants will depress the natural breath response. To a certain extent, the negative effects of these substances can be counteracted with a healthy life-style, but arranging one's life to minimize exposure and intake of these chemicals will allow for more freedom of the breath and consequently, less stress.

Activities which get the breath going are exercise, relaxation, and orgasmic responses. Hot or cold showers, running, swimming, deep breathing, pranayama, yoga, Reichian therapy, dancing, and sex are all good ways to get the breath going again.

Massage

We all know massage is an excellent way to get in touch with our bodies. During a good massage all the places that are tight and painful are revealed and given an opportunity to release. By adding your breath awareness you can aid the release of tight muscles and stuck energy.

Don't wait for your next massage appointment to get massaged. Touching your own body is another way to listen to it. We naturally rub our shoulders and eyebrows when they get tight. The Eastern health systems have developed self-massage to a high art-science, they have ways of kneading, beating, and stimulating acupressure points most of us have never dreamed of.

A special way to nurture yourself is a lotion rub before bed. After you bathe take a few minutes to rub your entire body with lotion Give your face, hands, and feet special attention because of the reflex points on those parts. If this is made into a nightly routine you will sleep better and have more youthful skin. The dryness that comes from hot tubbing, sun bathing, swimming in chlorine or salt water, or just plain bathing is counteracted by this delicious nightly habit.

The most important massage to do for yourself is stomach massage for healthy digestion. Massage in a clockwise direction, paying particular attention to stomach, liver, gall bladder, ileocecal valve, sigmoid flexure, the small intestine, and the entire length of the colon. Proper assimilation and elimination are essential for health and this is a very pleasant way to ensure good digestive tone.

Diet

Your body deserves only the best food. Pure energy foods are best when eaten whole, absolutely fresh, and minimally processed. Local foods are preferred to exotic foods flown in from other places because they are fresher and more attuned to your climate. Eating simply and paying attention to food combining will insure a healthy digestive tract and proper assimilation.

Commit yourself to a healthy, balanced, and natural diet. Whole grains, greens, succulent vegetables, fruit, sea vegetables, complete proteins, organic meat (if you eat meat), healthy fermented foods like yogurt and miso, and concentrated foods like Brewer's yeast and wheat grass juice are also desirable.

Because grounding is so important to the healer, the type of diet you eat may lean toward the yang foods: grains and beans, eggs and nut butters, squash and pumpkin. For some it feels better to eat meat. You have to sense where you are with your body.

I was vegetarian for nine years. I was careful about eating complete proteins, I didn't use sugar, coffee, or drugs, and I took a special yeast supplement that had B-12. I studied everything I could get my hands on about nutrition, especially vegetarian nutrition. It was not enough, I grew progressively weaker, spacier, and toxic. Finally I had to admit to myself that something was missing from my diet.

I experimented with eating fish and chicken. My health improved markedly and I have not had any problems since.

You must see what works for you. There are many vegetarians who thrive on that regime. But if you are doing bodywork, make sure your diet is going to help you stay grounded and healthy.

What are the substances that cut off your grounding? Anything yin, according to macrobiotic theory. That includes drugs, sugar, caffeine, alcohol, too much fruit and fasting, liquids (sodas, fruit juice, tea, etc.), and carbonated drinks. All of these substances (or practices) should be used in moderation or avoided entirely because they are so hard to balance.

Even the most health conscious people can overdo the yin foods. I knew a wonderful massage therapist who only ate pure foods, paid strict attention to food combining, and did regular colon cleansing. Her diet consisted of fruit, nuts, and seeds. She was full of light and love, but she could not remember appointments. She was very pure, but she was also very poor.

On the other end of the spectrum, what foods are too yang? Meat and salt. Especially beef, pork, lamb, and duck, Kentucky Fried Salt, chips, pickles, olives, cheese and all sausages. What foods clog your plumbing? All of the above and... fried foods, white bread, canned and frozen anything, complex combinations, too many different foods at once (potlucks and wedding receptions wreck havoc on your digestive system), anything containing artificial preservatives, emulsifiers, and dyes.

Mixing coffee, sugar, or alcohol with food is not a good idea because they block digestive enzymes. Coffee and chocolate tie up calcium which means you have bound calcium depositing in your muscles taking up space and causing havoc instead of being available for muscle contraction and bone repair.

The health of your colon is important. A regular cleansing regime, a variety and appropriate amount of fiber in your diet, cyclic exercise (walking, bicycling, running, swimming, aerobics), massage, generous doses of acidophilus, and acupressure will ensure the proper functioning of this most important organ.

Taking time out to cleanse the body of impurities at least once a year is important. Fasting with juices or brown rice for a few days is a good way to stimulate the immune system to eliminate toxins. It is suggested that you take a vacation while you fast so that you have a minimum of stress, lots of time to relax and nurture yourself in non-food ways, and allow the body and mind to process the toxins without you having to be "on" to do bodywork. When you are processing lots of toxins, you usually feel awful, tired, ugly, and nasty, anything but the alive, aware, grounded feeling you need to do bodywork.

If you have trouble fasting then you may benefit from eating a cleansing diet which is composed of vegetables, brown rice, miso, and tofu. You may also include raw salads with parsley, herbs, sprouts, lemon, olive oil, and lots of garlic. To keep yourself in protein eat nuts, seeds, and yogurt. The main idea is to keep your diet as simple and cleansing as possible, avoid mixing proteins and eat light.

This diet will keep your blood sugar stable and if followed for at least three days, the results are just as good as if you fasted.

I've also found having "fruit days" beneficial. When I'm a little under the weather, and my digestion feels overloaded, I'll eat fruit all day. The next day I feel just great.

As a detoxifier, nothing can beat pure delicious water. I suggest you get a water purifier if your water comes from anything but the purest source. Even streams and wells can contain contaminants and bacteria. Bottled water can contain algae and bacteria because it has no chlorine to stop their growth. Tap water does contain chlorine, fluorine, chloroforms, heavy metals, and various other substances you probably don't want in your body. If there isn't a distributor in your area, you can call or write me if you want information about water filters.

Eight glasses a day is the recommended amount. One way to make sure you drink that much is to fill up a bottle and carry it around with you.

Another wonderful detoxifier is chlorophyll. Wheat grass juice, spirulina, chlorella, and dark green vegetables are all good ways to take chlorophyll. Interestingly, the molecular structure of chlorophyll and hemoglobin (the oxygen carrier of blood) is almost identical. Fresh air and sunshine are also powerful detoxifiers. A hike in the woods or a visit to the beach has a very beneficial effect on depleted systems. Making it a habit to get out in nature will ensure a healthier body, mind, and spirit.

Taking a balanced attitude toward your diet doesn't mean you have to sacrifice. Eat well in daily life. Let yourself have pleasure food once in a while.

When you fall short of your ideals forgive yourself

instead of beating on yourself. For every gain you make, pat yourself on the back. Attitudes can be a lot more toxic than the food you eat.

CHAPTER SIX

PHYSICAL SELF-CARE

First Aid for Hands

You are a professional body therapist. You may have experienced some problems with your hands, and wonder whether you'll be able to keep on working if they give out. You would like to know how to help them feel better, but you don't want to take time out from making a living. How can you take care of yourself while you take care of others?

This next section is devoted to healing the hands of healers. It is a compilation of deep tissue massage techniques, strengthening regimes, and body awareness exercises which are used to treat sore hands. Some of these deep tissue manipulations you can do yourself, some with the aid of an experienced friend. They will help your injuries heal faster by putting the muscles back into their place of maximum work efficiency.

We will also make some simple suggestions for speeding up the healing process, but recommend you put yourself under the care of a competent chiropractor or osteopath that you trust. It is important to get an accurate diagnosis on your particular problem and to assure the vertebrae and the joints are in alignment. To aid my own healing process I have also used the services of acupuncturists and nutritional consultants.

The following soft-tissue manipulations are based on the work of Lauren Berry. They were given to me by Dan Harvey, who is my favorite body mechanic. His mentor, Lauren Berry, formed a school of bodywork that combined osteopathic manipulations, sports massage technique, and lymphatic drainage. I find it a comprehensive system and adhere to many of its theoretical principles in my own work.

There are four principles we are working with here that are important to understand before attempting these muscle manipulations.

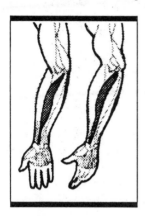

One is that **every muscle has a position** between its insertion and origin, and in relation to the muscles surrounding it that is its best position, i.e. working efficiency is at its maximum in this position. Most muscles operate in a groove nestled in between adjoining muscles, tendons, and bone structure. The muscle slides up and down in this groove as it works.

The second principle is that **muscles have direction**, and if you push the muscle back into its groove, in a balanced place between the insertion and origin, it will relax and work more efficiently. The way you sense the muscle direction is by palpation or muscle testing. The resistant direction or weak test is the way you do not want to push the muscle back into the groove. Generally, but not always, the right direction is the one in which the muscle yields gratefully to being eased back into its maximum position. Exceptions will

be complicating factors (such as an obstructing ligament), techniques using cross-grain, and trigger point massage. I prefer the less painful techniques and only use the more painful ones if gentle manipulation is not working. Knowledge of how a muscle is located with respect to other muscles is imperative. Keep an anatomy chart or book nearby so you can refer to it when necessary. Muscle testing will reveal information you need if palpation does not.

The third principle is that **muscles have layers**. The superficial layers are generally broader and flatter than the deeper layers. If you release the superficial layers of tissue first, and then address the next layer, your work will be much easier, and more comfortable for the recipient.

The fourth principle is that muscle groups carry a **line of tension** from the origin of the pressure or work applied to the core structure. It is more thorough to release a muscle and then check the muscles in kinesthetic relationship to it, so that you are sure the entire line of tension is released.

The most important rule to remember is respect the body you are working on. Know your anatomy and range of movements. Be firm and decided in your touch. Also know exactly what each manipulation accomplishes. Do not force any joint in a way it does not work, or you will damage the joint.

Thumbs

The opponis pollicis longus has a tendency to rotate toward the palm when we exert a lot of pressure on them. Grab the opponis pollicis longus at the tendon line and work them back to where they've migrated from.

Fingers

The extensor and digital tendons will rotate medially also. Unravel them and rotate laterally.

When the capsules between the joints in the fingers slip out of place, you will experience tenderness when pressing the joint. Place the first joint of your index finger underneath the line of the joint you are treating. This is your fulcrum. Gradually lift joint, and guide capsule back into place.

Wrists

Carpals usually pop straight out. Gap the wrist by grabbing it underneath the metacarpals on either side and pull gently on the wrist. Guide the carpal bone back into place.

It's important to keep the carpal bones in their correct position because they will cause dysfunction and inflammation in the ligamental cuff which can pinch the nerve running underneath it. This will cause a lot of pain up and down the arm if they are not attended to. Correct realignment of carpal bones will help clear up carpal tunnel syndrome, especially if all other dysfunctions are addressed.

Added note by author: I have found an adjustment to the elbows, shoulders, and then the cervical and thoracic spine are helpful in correcting carpal tunnel syndrome. Even if the origin of the injury is in the wrist, compensation can cause dysfunction in the arm musculature, shoulder placement, and the spinal curve between the scapula. It is a good idea to check them for proper alignment and full range of movement to see if this is the case.

Elbow

Often pain and tenderness is experienced just below the elbow. Check the notches on either side of the elbow. It may feel as if the carti-

lage is bulging out, and the place will be tender. You will be able to feel it as a soft ridge. Gap the joint and press the cartilage back in. For tennis elbow, press laterally. For the lateral epicondyle

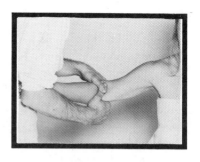

anconeus

groove, gap medial (see illustration), press cartilage into joint, and straighten arm to lock in place. Check the seating of the radius and the ulna. A kneading massage from wrist to elbow around the bones will help gently guide them back so that there is free range of movement in the elbow. Commonly the brachioradialis, flexor longus pollicis, and the supinator brevis will need some deep tissue, as will the flexor profundus digitorum. Note that if there is tension in the pronator teres (you will feel a band of tissue underneath the brachioradialis), deep tissue along the insertion of the anconeus (opposite side of forearm) is a more comfortable and effective method of release. This is a fairly common dysfunction.

Shoulders

The deltoids will rotate anteriorly and often the bicep tendon will roll out of its groove on the

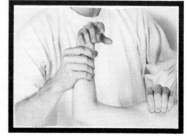

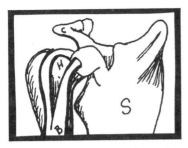

out of its groove on the shoulder. You will be able to palpate the head of the bicep. It will feel like a taut rope. Move the deltoid up (cranially) and out (dorsally). Lift the bicep tendon back up into its groove. The anterior deltoid most often falls down, so lift it cranially. The pectorals can be addressed while the recipient is lying on their side, by grasping the muscle at the origin and moving it laterally while moving the shoulder to open and stretch the muscle. It is also possible to address them anteriorly while the recipient is on their back. It is easier to work deeply with the attachment to the collarbone in this position.

Generally, the rotator cuffs drop down, but as always check the direction. Four muscles go to make up the rotator cuff: the teres minor, infra- and supraspinatus and subscapularis. Push them toward their origins.

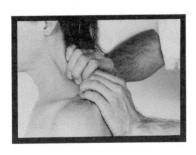

Because we are standing at a table and applying pressure out and downward, the upper trapezius will have a tendency to move (cranially) up and (ventrally) over the shoulder girdle. Grasp them firmly with a maximum of surface pressure and rotate them medially at a 45% angle to the spine.

Back

Begin at the first layer and push the lower trapezius cranially and laterally. Push the rhomboids laterally and caudally toward the scapula, and with a circular directional motion (cranially and laterally) tease the spinalis dorsi out from between the vetebrae. Release the latis- 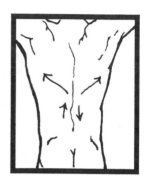 simus dorsi by pushing cranially and laterally toward the edge of the scapula, and check the anterior and posterior serratus muscles. If they feel swollen and tender, use the broad part of your palm to knead them cranially and laterally.

Check the quadratus for muscle direction (this is not consistent from person to person!) and adjust for maximum position. For example, on someone who uses their right hand a lot to do deep work, their back muscles will go down on the right side and up on the left. You will need to move them in the opposite direction in order to balance them.

Recovery

The best treatment for injured soft tissue is rest and ice. I have found acupuncture applied to the injured tissue helpful for relieving pain and edema. Taking a calcium-magnesium supplement with synergistic vitamins and enzymes speeded up the recovery when I needed to rebuild tissue. Deep slow acupressure, applied daily, will increase the circulation to the injury.

Amica is an inexpensive homeopathic remedy for muscular strain, and comes in a cream, gel, or oil base. I have found direct application on the tissue worked better for me than taking the pills.

Deep, slow acupressure

Chinese herbal medicine has developed analgesic plasters which are applied directly to the injured area and worn all day to help ease the pain.

The most powerful technological tools for rapid recovery are ultrasound and the acuscope. Ultrasound is good for improving circulation in inflamed tissue, and the acuscope stimulates tissue to heal by passing a small electrical current through the tissue. Many chiropractors have ultrasound, and the acuscope is becoming more popular, but you may have to look harder to find it. A sports clinic or a chiropractor which specializes in sports injuries may have one. The acuscope runs a very mild current between two electrodes which you apply directly to the skin along with an electrolytic gel.

Strenghtening

Once the tissue is healed, a series of strengthening exercises will prevent further injury. Some good strength-

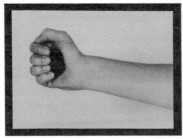

ening tools are hand presses, rubber balls (for squeezing), clubs for swinging, and Baoding balls to increase finger dexterity, strength, and forearm flexibility.

Rubber ball

Weight-training will increase the overall body strength. Nautilus equipment is good because it is based on resistance training, which is the same type of force as we apply in the session.

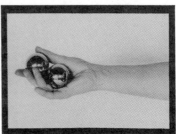

Baoding balls

Aerobic yoga will also improve body strength and can be substituted for weight training.

As you get stronger, move from the first level to the second.

1st Level: Downward-facing dog

2nd Level: Crow pose

Strokes to Watch Out for During the Session

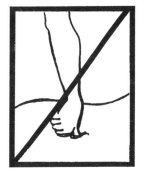

Thumb drilling - Thumbs are usually the first anatomical part to wear out. Most body therapies use the thumb because it is such a handy instrument—it has great sensitivity and a broad strong base joint for exerting pressure. But too much repeated pressure can cause damage to the synovial membrane in the thumb joint, which leads to swelling and inflammation.

Solutions:

1. Bracing the thumb with the other thumb, hand, or elbow will give that joint extra strength and support.
2. When working on the back, moving up the spine, brace hands together, so the thumbs support each other.
3. Use your thumb as sensor, so that you can use a stronger body part, like the elbow, to exert pressure.
4. Use the mound of your hand right under the thumb on the legs and arms. Be careful not to compress your wrist.

5. The forearm and the elbow can be substituted for thumb in most situations that involve large areas.

Wrist compression - Wrists are the next most common injury in bodywork and massage therapy. Compressing the wrist can cause damage to the synovial membranes, dislocation of the carpal bones with each other, the metacarpals, and the ulna, and wearing down of the capsular, interosseous, and lateral ligaments.

1. Always keep wrist in alignment so weight is evenly distributed while applying pressure.

2. Build up the strength in forearm with weight training and yoga practices listed in this book.

3. Avoid torquing movements when applying pressure.

Torquing - All movements involving pressure and a twist can wrench the joints of the wrist, elbow, and shoulder. Torquing without pressure for light strokes is OK. Torquing with the body instead of the wrist allows you to follow the natural body lines of the client.

Shoulders up - When you have to lift your shoulders to get the right pressure over a place in a client's body you compromise your own body. Change your body position so that your vector of force is translated through your entire body.

1. Use your whole body for each stroke.
2. Be physically grounded without being rigid. A common mistake is to plant the feet as if they were roots. This restricts free movement and can injure the back. Every time you move, your feet should reflect the movement.
3. Be aware of the sensations in your shoulder joint. If you feel yourself straining, stop, shift your position so you are using the joint to its greatest advantage. This will prevent damage to the ligaments of the shoulder joints.

Gripping with the feet - In lieu of grounding, a common mistake is to use tension in the feet to brace yourself when executing strong strokes.

Grounding with your energy, relaxing your feet and staying sensually connected with the earth will help keep you from slipping. Working on carpet or sticky mats is better than a slippery floor. When traveling it is a good idea to carry a sticky mat in case your client has hardwood floors.

Lifting heavy clients can cause damage to the lower back, the tendons under the forearm, and the anterior tendons of the shoulder joint. These tendons can drop out of their grooves and cause a fiery pain in the front of the shoulder which is difficult to massage out. The tendons need to be returned to their grooves. This is a common injury among people who work with weights, or do a lot of heavy lifting in their job.

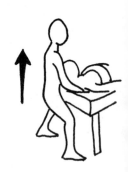

1. Always lift with your legs (even if it's just your client's shoulder). This will protect your back. Watch for stretching and bending the torso.
2. Strong muscles will protect the tendons under the forearm. If you are not already well-developed, strengthening exercises will protect your wrists.
3. Find ways to lift body parts that involve leverage instead of physical strength.

Stretching and bending the torso can lead to low back pain at places of negotiation. Try to use the body as a whole unit, avoid contorted positions.

Compressed buttocks - Bringing the pelvis forward and bracing against the table is a bad habit. You limit your movement to only the upper part of the body, create blockage and tension in your buttocks and

hamstrings. Get a sense of where your bones are when you work. Let your skeleton support your muscles in their work. This will keep you focused on your alignment.

Neck gymnastics - Holding the head up while working on the back creates tension in the back of the neck. Keep the neck in line with the spine as much as possible.

Knee locks - Pressing knees back or holding them still in horse stance can put strain on the knees. Keep knees fluid. Let the legs move with the stroke.

Fighting tense muscles - One of the most powerful techniques for deep tissue massage is putting the muscle in slack before going in. If the muscle is tensed, you must work very hard to get the muscle to relax, but if you gently push the adjacent joint in, it puts the muscle in its relaxed position and softens it. The muscle will not be able to tense against your pressure.

How Aston-Patterning Changed My Life

In everyone's life there are events that take place which seem unfortunate when viewed from the outside. However, if we examine the resulting chain of events that the "misfortune" sets in motion, we realize it was a "happy accident."

My happy accident was injuring my right arm by doing deep tissue work intensively (and incorrectly) for five years. The injury was so bad that it impaired my ability to do bodywork. The pain was excruciating, my shoulder throbbed, my wrist hurt constantly, and a chronic misalignment in my back sent shooting pains down my arm.

Every time I did a session I was tormented by the pain, but I loved doing bodywork. I considered changing professions, but my heart wanted to do bodywork. After a great deal of inner struggle, I realized I had to change the way I used my body so my job would not hurt my body. I sought out other professionals who could help me learn how to use my body without injuring myself.

The person who was most instrumental in this learning process was Judith Aston. I took her Aston Massage course in January 1987, and much of the material in this chapter is derived from her workshop. The remainder came from my original teacher, Fred Mitouer, bodywork sessions with Dan Harvey, innumerable conversations with chiropractors and sports injury specialists, and my martial arts training.

Judith helped me see the body in a whole new conceptual framework. The experiential part of the workshop was invaluable kinesthetic information for me as a bodyworker and I highly recommend taking the course firsthand if at all possible. Judith's understanding of the body and the way it works is superb, especially on the levels of micro-movement, directionality of tissue, and physical kinesthetics.

With Judith's help, I was not only able to fix the arm, but also eliminate the cause, which was the use of static force instead of the efficient use of gravity with my body.

Aston-Patterning is an integrative system that focuses on the body as a dynamic structure involved in a variety of activities within an environmental milieu.

The body is not considered in isolation, nor is it forced into a paradigm of perfect structural balance.

The purpose of Aston-Patterning is to educate the client in **how to use their body with greater efficiency and just the right amount of tension for the task**. It helps the person to increase their range of choices so that **they can respond with more fluidity** to the shapes of objects they use and the energetic demands in their environment. In addition to the soft tissue work the Aston method incorporates movement education, environmental modification, and fitness training.

I learned that for the bodyworker, as well as the client, the session can be an active arena for learning and personal growth. Every session deepens our understanding of human bodies and allows us ample opportunity to study the effect of mind and emotions on the body's structure. Watching our own bodies and minds while we do bodywork will help us work efficiently and gracefully. Bodyworkers can and do get hurt when they use their bodies incorrectly. Moving with consciousness makes physical injury much less likely to occur.

Learning to do bodywork well is a meditation on body/mind coordination, much like T'ai Chi. We can pick up the correct positions for the arms and legs in a couple of months, but years pass before we can claim to know the form. When we graduated from school and got our certificate our education had just begun. It takes many years to learn how to get the desired result **effortlessly.**

The untrained mind will turn off the thinking mind to conserve energy, but this is not always to your advantage. How many times have you walked from one room to the next and forgotten what you came for? You had a thought, "Oh, I need a pencil." You get up and move your body to another location, going from a thinking mode to a kinesthetic mode. There is a break in the continuity of the thought when you switched modes. If we train our minds to stay engaged while we move, we can not only remember what we came into the next room for, (a useful skill indeed!), we can also improve our bodywork.

The key to graceful, efficient and conscious body movement is learning to move in rhythm with the breath. In T'ai Chi the mind is being trained to concentrate on coordinating the body and the breath so that they move as a unit. The mind is gently guided away from distracting thoughts and sensations so it may focus on the body.

The T'ai Chi practitioner develops the ability to concentrate *and* breathe at the same time. It's much like the trick of rubbing one's stomach while patting the head, a little difficult at first, but with practice it can be done.

In the bodywork session coordinating our breathing with our movements helps us focus our attention on the interaction between our body and that of our client. When we are able to concentrate on the body and mind simultaneously, bodywork becomes an energy-releasing meditation.

Burnout happens when we are expending energy faster than our systems can handle it. The power to release energy through the breath regenerates us while we work. It is a sure prevention against burnout. We can create the desired transformations in our clients without getting depleted.

By making bodywork a meditation, we can become more sensitive to subtle kinesthetic relationships during a session. Which techniques feel effortless, which cause pain and create resistance?

Bodies are very intelligent; pain is teaching us what to avoid. You can learn to use pain as a signal that you need to change what you are doing. If the technique is causing pain in your body, you are doing something off-center. Be sensitive to your client's pain as well. Some clients will not tell you when they are feeling pain. They will grimace, tighten up, or fight back, long before they will admit they are feeling pain.

For the bodyworker, an awkward position, a mis-alignment, or even just a negative thought which activates our emotional holding pattern can cause us physical pain. Ignoring the pain can lead to a serious injury. If we acknowledge the pain, it is possible to trace it to the cause and then we can do something about the pain.

Pain taught me something very valuable about my body. It was the fifth year of my deep tissue practice that I developed problems with my wrist and elbow. Due to the chronic stress created by wrist compression com-bined with a torquing motion, the ulna had rotated and partially dislocated. This pushed my carpal bones out of alignment, and in sympathetic response, my hu-merus dislocated at the shoulder joint. My subscapu-laris and teres minor were consequently in chronic spasm, which cut off the circulation to my hands and the resulting tension caused me to lose my thoracic curve and the nerves between T-3,4,5 were pinched.

I had developed carpal tunnel syndrome, a com-mon complaint among bodyworkers. Every time I did a session my arm ached and a line of fire burned under the carpal ligaments.

I was able to get the bones back into place, but the chronic stress had weakened and stretched the liga-ments. Whenever I exerted pressure on them in a certain direction the bones would slip out again. I was forced to cut back my client load to give my arm a rest.

For my next step, I developed a set of strengthening exercises and muscle balancing movements to accompany the physical therapy, and changed the way I did bodywork so I didn't have to use physical strength.

Judith Aston helped me find two strokes in my shoulder sequence that were causing the problem. One involved standing at the client's head and pressing down on their shoulder with a torquing motion. The other stroke was one which opened up the back of the client's shoulder beautifully, but put excessive strain on my lumbar spine and carpal ligaments.

Judith helped me develop an alternate stroke for the torquing stroke and changed my foot position for the second stroke. The pain went away and only returns when I need to be reminded to be conscious.

I received a great gift from the pain in my arm. I improved the way I did bodywork because I was forced into growing out of my set way of doing things. It stimulated me to research self-care for bodyworkers and to write this book. Learning new techniques brought a lightness and freshness into my bodywork and expanded my awareness of my own body.

The Bodyworker's Toolbox

In addition to our hands, we also have breath, motion, falling, weight, vectors of force, centering, and grounding to use as tools. We can focus on these during the session to help us keep the energy flowing strongly and use our bodies in the most efficient manner.

Breath - Deep breathing energizes the blood which gives the body strength. Blood carries the oxygen necessary for aerobic muscular activity, electrical charges for healthy chemical reactions and stimulates cellular respiration. Deep breathing keeps your mind alert and focused, and encourages the client to deepen their breathing.

Keeping the breath going is crucial for the body-worker. During the session, there will be times when we need to concentrate. Our unconscious reaction is to hold our breath while we think. Whenever we do this, we cut off the flow of chi, the healing energy flowing through our bodies.

If you find this happening while you are working just exhale, a deep breath will follow naturally. Full deep breathing will keep our energy at a high level even though the work day is long.

Motion - The tendency with a particularly difficult place on a client is to slow down or stop so we can concentrate on the body part. But the client responds on a subconscious level to us; if we've stopped, they've probably stopped too. If you feel stuck, check to see if you've frozen a portion of your body or stopped moving altogether. Try moving your whole body and see if that increases the client's ability to let go.

Falling - When we are at work, we spend much of our time leaning forward. Gravity is with us. It is not necessary to use a lot of muscle to create a lot of change or to work up a sweat. If we allow ourselves to fall into the tissue, it is much more comfortable for the client and it's easier on our bodies. The tenderest muscle can accept a lot of pressure if it is applied slowly and sensitively. Our clients are more likely to let us in if they don't feel forced to let go.

Surrender is a big part of the healing process, especially for bodyworkers with big egos. We may have the technique and strength to fix misalignments, but unless there is patience on our parts and voluntary surrender on the client's part, the misalignments usually come back. Unless our clients have made the necessary mental adjustments they will not sustain the physical changes. Clients are more likely to let you work deeply if they trust you not to cause unnecessary pain. They appreciate your caring and sympathy and it helps them feel better about being in their bodies.

Weight - Following right on the heels of the subject of falling is weight. By using our weight more, we use our muscles less. That might mean changing our foot position, finding ways to use gravity as a tool, or getting a straight vector of force over the client.

The most effective way to use our weight (instead of our strength) is to use our whole body for every stroke, even the little ones. While we are working, let's watch for ways we work against ourselves. Is our whole body behind our stroke? Is there any part going in another direction or bracing? Are we working against ourselves? **If every movement is a whole body movement, all the force gets focused like a laser. It's very powerful.**

Getting the whole body behind the stroke might mean changing foot placement. For example, if you are covering a large area of the body and going from one height to another, planting your feet in a fixed stance is going to pull on ligaments and destroy the effectiveness of the stroke. Balancing on one foot and moving off of the other gives the stroke three-dimensionality. This gives our bodies a greater range of movement and can focus the body's weight in the direction of the stroke.

To get our weight over the client so we can use gravity, we can change our height. A step, or some high heel clogs you can slip into will give us the added inches when we are working on the highest parts of the client.

Turning the client on his or her side to work on the back allows us to use our weight better. Instead of having to get up and over the client, we can work on a diagonal. It is easier to maintain our alignment, we have to cover less distance, and we minimize the stretching and bending movements that cause muscle strain.

If we find we are using force, but don't know how to put our body in a position that uses our whole weight, we can correct that by visualizing our vector of force.

Vectors of force - If the body is used as an integral unit, as it is when you use your weight properly, the vector of force from your feet to your hands will form an unbroken line.

A broken vector of force means that some part of our body is working against us. We are splitting our weight, or compromising a part of our body. At the place of negotiation, tension sets up. We may not feel any pain at the time, but a repeated pattern of using our bodies incorrectly causes chronic stress which wears away at the integrity of the compromised body part. The injury can come on slowly or suddenly, but once it happens it impairs our ability to do good work.

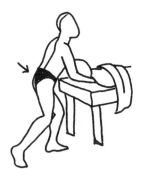

Centering - Moving from our center of gravity will help us to use your bodies correctly.

If you have a low center of gravity, you can get powerful movements using your legs, people with a high center of gravity can use their shoulders more.

Sensing when we are moving from our center takes attention, time, and practice. All the martial arts teach the student to originate movement from the center. Tradition locates this center right under the belly button. The Chinese call it the "t'an tien," the Japanese call it the "hara."

The center is the seat of all emotion, passion, and motivation. To generate motion from this center means that your whole body is behind the movement. There is less tendency to resist or perform incomplete movements when we come from center. When we are intimately in touch and balanced with our kinesthetic sense, there is much less chance that we will hurt ourselves or our client. Center is the place of maximum effective movement and sensitivity.

Distracting thoughts will pull your energy out of your center and into your head. Unresolved emotions create physical blocks in the body which affect alignment and interfere with a clear flow of energy (refer to vector of force). To get fully behind any physical movement we should be focused on what we are doing.

Grounding

What is grounding? I hear bodyworkers talk about grounding all the time, the visualizations that they do, their lack of it, that a little excess weight helps them stay grounded, how hugging a tree helps their grounding, this or that crystal helps their grounding, this or that healer is so grounded, but what is this mysterious quality?

For the purposes of this book we define grounding as a fluid and unimpaired connection with the earth. Physically, it is having our legs relaxed, in balance with an even tone. In Aikido, it is called weight underside. Emotionally, it is ease, confidence and comfort with being in a body. Mentally, it's an alive, alert, aware attitude so that we can respond quickly and appropriately to events in our lives.

Grounded is not a heavy feeling. Quite the opposite, it's relaxed and springy. When we are in balance with gravity, we have just the right amount of tension in our bodies, no more, no less. All unnecessary tension is released and the muscles are working in harmony with each other.

Learning how to relax our musculature in the right places will give our movements an effortless quality because we are no longer fighting gravity, we are working with it. For a bodyworker, having a grounded, relaxed, and balanced body greatly facilitates our work with other people.

After the Session

Stretching - Stretching out between sessions allows us to breathe a bit, get rid of any tension we may have picked up and to compose our minds for the next client. The following stretches can be done on the floor or a massage table and are particularly good for bodyworkers as they address the wrists, forearms, shoulders, and back muscles used in the session.

Bend over at hips and hang over legs.

Spread legs wide and bend over with head hanging.

Swing arms to open back of shoulders between scapula.

Spread legs wide and bend over with hands clasped behind back.

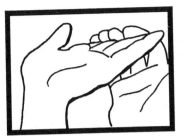 

Stretch palm up.   Stretch top of hand.

Rotate wrists.   Shake gently to release
                         excess energy.

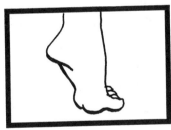 

Open feet with toe   Open feet by pressing
stretches. Pay attention heel to ground as you
to alignment.   stretch forward.

Exercise - Exercising at the end of our work day
effectively releases muscular and mental tension,
gets rid of aggressions and frustrations, and helps
the body to relax so we get adequate rest for the next
day. If you have the energy, yoga or running is good
exercise. If you are too tired, the stretches alone will
help relax you and restore balance to your body.

Restorative Poses

Lie on table or floor. For opening heart, diaphragm and hips.

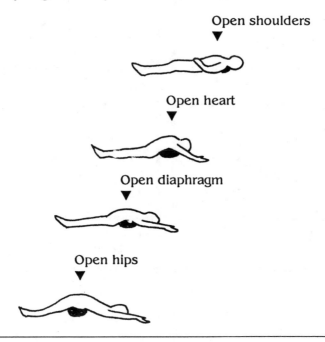

Open shoulders
▼

Open heart
▼

Open diaphragm
▼

Open hips
▼

Supine Balls

Tie two balls together in a sock.

Start at the bottom of your spine and work your way up by moving 1" for each vertebrae.

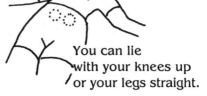

You can lie with your knees up or your legs straight.

CHAPTER SEVEN

PSYCHOLOGICAL SELF-CARE

Empathy

Have you ever felt yourself getting sick around sick people? Feeling sad because others are sad? Irritated because someone next to you is angry? Have you ever wondered why this happens?

Empathy occurs when we mirror another person's thoughts and emotions. It is a common occurrence: children, dogs, and plants all respond unreservedly to their emotional environment. How many times have we responded with agitation when the baby starts to fuss? Snapped back at a rude motorist? Cried at a sad movie? It is natural to feel affected by our surroundings. We are constantly responding on a subconscious level to the environment which surrounds us. Every time we interact with others, we take in cues from their facial expressions, dress, body language, skin, and voice quality. We sense things about them, drawing information about them by their sounds, colors, textures, and smells. Most of these cues are completely subliminal and never even register with our conscious minds. However if we are sensitive to our internal world, we will notice what goes on in our subconscious minds and see when there is a contrast to what is occurring outside. This ability to hold both realities at once will enable us to respond more appropriately than if we only paid attention to the "obvious" reality.

When we enter into empathy with another person, it's just like tuning into a radio station—we pick up signals about their state of being and play it through our minds. In the body therapy session, we may find ourselves responding to our client's emotion, and thinking thoughts which do not seem our own. Since many of the people who come to us are not feeling well, when we interact with them and touch them, a lot of so-called "negative" information (fear, rage, lust, judgement, etc.) is being processed by our subconscious minds.

Empathy with clients is a phenomena which psychotherapists often deal with. Although it can be useful to the treatment process, empathy can also lead to emotional burnout if the psychotherapist is not careful with their boundaries.

As body therapists, we come in intimate contact with the client's emotional body at a touch level. It is a primal, pre-verbal stage of emotional need. There may be huge barriers to getting touched, and conversely, an endless aching hunger for touch. The kinds of touch a client may be able to tolerate will be colored by painful associations. An auto accident or sexual abuse can leave a client too sensitive for anything but the lightest stroking.

To protect ourselves from taking on our client's psychological imprint we need to recognize a subliminal unconscious informational exchange is taking place, and learn how to manage the input.

When we find ourselves taking on an uncomfortable or foreign emotional state, we need to make a mental separation in our mind between ourselves and our clients.

We need to keep that mental separation active throughout the session, and clear ourselves emotionally when they leave. We'll find as we let go of our own psychological baggage, we are less willing to add someone else's to our load.

To make the mental separation, we need to know

our own emotional makeup well enough to distinguish it from that of our client's. We learn to identify feelings which are "not-self" feelings, much like the body's immune system learns to identify "not-self" proteins.

At first, making the separation is difficult because we get caught up in the force of our emotions. However, once the separation process is set in motion, it gets easier to identify "not-self" emotions. The more we practice this, the more expertise we gain at recognizing and handling foreign feelings as they arise. Over time, we build up an immunity to "not-self" feelings. The way I make the necessary mental separation is to say to myself, "I am not my client and their problems are not mine, no matter how similar they may seem."

When you first start making this mental separation, you may encounter a problem with "professional guilt." This is a mental trap healers often fall into. If the client is not healing at the expected rate, it can throw us off emotionally. There are times when we will feel inadequate and that we lack the knowledge, technique, and insight to handle this client. We would like to be omniscient, but we are not always going to know what to do. We need to accept that we are doing our best—given our current store of knowledge, vitality levels, and ability to see inside the situation. Even if our clients are not getting better, that is all we can do.

When we feel guilty, we are leaving ourselves wide open to pick up our client's unwanted emotions. Instead of moving them out, we are just moving the emotions to another place.

Unless you have done something really wrong, like sexually abuse your client, or misuse your power of authority, feelings of professional guilt usually are not founded in reality.

First of all, we're not the party responsible for the healing.

It is our clients who have the power to heal, not us. The client chose to come to us and has confidence in us. The choice to heal is the beginning of all healing. The power of that choice lies in their hands, not ours. **When we see our clients as capable, that advances the empathy into heart-felt compassion**.

I had a client that I worked on for two years who never got better. She was wild about my work and sent me all kinds of clients, but I never could get her to move out of her pain and negative emotions. I tried everything—deep tissue, laying on of hands, psychic counseling, orthobionomy, hypnosis—everything that is, except seeing her as healed. Then I had a dream about her as she could be: whole, well, out of physical and emotional pain, productive, involved in a career she loved, with harmonious relationships. I went into the next session with this vision in mind, and she got not only got better, she changed careers and moved to Hawaii with her husband, which is something she always wanted to do.

We may help them feel faith in their healing process. We may provide an environment which healing can take place. We may even shamanistically "trick" the client out of believing in their illness, but it is the client that does the healing.

Healing is a growing process, even when the body is repairing damage. It is an intrinsic process. It takes time, and moves at its own pace. How can we facilitate this process?

Nurture it, fertilize it, support it, water it regularly.

How do we handle our urges to control the situation? Relax, have patience.

It is just as important that we make the mental separation between our own psychological baggage and theirs. When I start a session, I will do a short guided relaxation along with my client that helps us put aside the outside world.

Let's take a deep breath together. With the next deep breath, let go of everything it took to get here. And with the next deep breath, let go of everything that happened today. With the next deep breath, let go of all the events of the week.

Impatience with the healing process is like pulling up the carrot to see how fast it's growing. Trust in the healing process; much of it takes place underneath the obvious reality, beyond what we can see. Trying to push things faster than they will go will give you momentary insight, but it's not good for the carrot.

Feelings

Strong emotions arise during the session. You feel a trickle of sweat under your arms because you are afraid of the amount of (rage, sadness, hysteria) being released, and you're afraid of your neighbors complaining about the noise. Take a deep breath. The best thing you can **do** now is help your client **be** with the emotions.

Words like "I'm here. You can hold my hand" are simple and effective. Offer them a kleenex for their eyes and nose if they need it. Acknowledge the feeling: "It's OK to say that here. Let it out. From what you've said since the session started, it sounds like the past week has been hard for you." It helps a lot to match your words to the client's emotional reality, the client feels heard and understood. It's important not to make them feel judged, or patronized. Avoid preaching at this moment.

Suppose you have strong feelings arise. Be honest,

but tactful. Admit how you feel. "I'm sorry, I don't feel comfortable after...(whatever upset you.) I'm not sure I can work on you now." Communications are a learned skill, so if you make mistakes, don't feel bad. You've learned something new about communicating with clients.

Suppose you feel lost. Ask the client, "Now where are we going? What would you like to have worked on?" This is empowering for the client, because they often have special areas of pain they want worked on.

We want to avoid intellectual identification with our client's problems, which is the official definition for empathy. Trying to solve their problems for them, glossing over their feelings because they are too much like our own, or feeling so deeply so that we take on their emotions and lose our sense of self will not help them.

Most of us are not licensed psychotherapists, or physicians. We are not required to solve our client's problems. Even psychotherapists don't do that. They can help their clients integrate emotions into a cognitive framework so the client can deal with them better, but psychotherapists do not solve their problems.

However, when strong emotions arise, there is nothing so powerful or healing as just being there: present in the moment, breathing, making eye contact, and emptying the mind of advice, judgement, and recipes for successful conclusions for the client while they go through their tears, laughter, and anger.

Clients are in a very vulnerable state when they are on the table: medical opinions, unsolicited advice, even compliments on the appearance of their bodies, can be misconstrued, so be careful.

Helping the client to deal successfully with these emotions and memories is not always an easy task, most of us are not trained counselors. Some of us may not want to spend the session time digging up old bad feelings. But if a deeply buried emotion erupts in the process of working on a client, this will help to free the body. Unless our practice is centered around emotional release and we have specific techniques for handling strong feelings, **all we need to do is be present with our clients** while they are re-experiencing these feelings. Compassion is one of the most powerful tools we have as healers.

Taking some courses in counseling may give us techniques for dealing with our client's emotions, but it is important to remember that our job is freeing the body. What we do for the heart and soul, we do mainly through touch, and it's good to keep the client's attention on what's happening in the body.

The best preparation for this type of work is doing our own private emotional process. It helps us get used to the waves of emotions without being inundated by them.

Confronting our own feelings helps us to know ourselves and clearly define our emotional patterns. Knowing ourselves and accepting ourselves allows us to have patience and compassion for others and what they are going through. Acknowledging our feelings helps them acknowledge their feelings, which is an important part of the healing process.

Having faced the wounds—the hurts done us and the hurts done by us—helps us help others face their hurts. Emotional clearing means finding a way to unearth our past hurts and work through them. Emotional clarity means freedom, because we are no longer suppressing our feelings or being controlled by our past, we are working with deep powerful sources in ourselves.

Wounded Healers

Bodyworkers are often motivated to take up a healing profession by a desire to "do good works." What is underneath this desire?

Under the surface of an altruist, we will often find a wound. At one time this person felt powerless, unwanted, or abandoned, probably at a very young age, and is determined to make up for that injustice. Carl Jung had a name for this type of person—he called them the "wounded healers."

For better or worse, being wounded attracts wounded people to us, often with a similar kind of wound. There is a chance for great healing if that wound is acknowledged, but there is the danger of getting caught in reinforcing habitual patterns if it is not. The thought I hold in my mind as I work is "May we both be healed."

I had a client who had so many problems she didn't know what to do or where to start. I worked with her for months, and ended up in one session listening to the very same problems that I had heard months before. I felt frustrated, discouraged, nothing had worked. I felt like a failure.

I stopped, took a deep breath and went inside to get guidance. "Stop trying so hard," my inner voice told me. "Don't solve all her problems for her. All she needs is a good massage." I did just that. The session drew to a close, the client got off the table, and dressed without saying a word. "How do you feel?" I asked her. She turned around, her face was radiant. "Great. Why do you ask?" she replied.

There is a resistant part in all of us that tries to keep the wounds from healing. We get used to doing things a certain way and sabotage well-intentioned attempts to change bad habits. I often have this strange feeling with certain clients that the same block keeps running around the body, masquerading as a shoulder pain, stomach pain, and tension in the feet, but it's really just one block, resistance to a frightening change. Like a little gremlin in the engine, gleefully it spreads havoc, agitation, and chaos while dodging our attempts to free the person of pain. The best way to defeat the "gremlin" is not to battle with them. Going to war against them adds more energy to the fear and resistance.

Instead, look for the new insight. Solicit your client's help in the process. Find the burning question. What's at risk? Bring light to the issue that is up and causing the resistance.

If we have driven out our own "demons" with the light of self-awareness, and are devoted to the process of healing our own wounds, we will be better guides along the healing path.

Love Addictions and Codependency

The best psychological protection I know is loving ourselves. All of us want to be loved and needed, but for some of us love addiction is all we know. When we love someone who can't return that love it creates a certain kind of obsession. These people can't give you love because they don't love themselves. The loved ones may be drug addicts, criminals, food addicts, alcoholics, workaholics, TVholics, rockaholics, religionholics, spacecases, or maybe they are just shut off from their feelings. Loving these people is not unhealthy (sometimes we don't have a choice), but sometimes the way we love them is a little crazy.

The definition of addiction is "engaging in compulsive behavior(s) in which we have no control." The way we know we are addicted is we can't stop ourselves. Even if we want to stop ourselves, we just can't do it.

My love addiction manifested as not being able stop myself from helping needy people, whether they wanted the help or not. Most of the time, they wanted the help, I was an easy pushover for a favor or community service. But I also had definite ideas about what was good for people and I couldn't leave someone who was hurting themselves alone. I had to help them out. I had quite a few drug addicts really mad at me for interfering with their right to enjoy their addiction.

What helped me to stop harming myself and others with my love addiction was to understand the origin of addiction, and unhook myself from the maladaptive behavior so I had a choice.

When I was a child, I witnessed an injustice being done and I was powerless to stop it. I bought the idea at a very young age that I was weak and stupid. I felt ashamed of my powerlessness, so I overcompensated by being loving. I loved everything and everybody ... indiscriminately. Because of my lack of discrimination I ended up getting beaten up, robbed, threatened, used, betrayed, and abused. I was a very sweet and loving person, and I was a target. What I lacked was love for myself.

The key to ending my love addiction was accepting myself totally as I am and loving myself without reservation. There are things which I would like to change about myself, yet it doesn't bother me that I'm not perfect.

Learning to love myself has been a long process. It means facing all the hurt that has been done to me and all the hurt I have done to others. It means facing my shame, rage, and grief, digging up parts of my past I'd rather forget and keep buried. It means saying "no" to people who don't understand why I'm not a "nice" person anymore. And it means letting go of controlling other people's lives. It means that I have to let go of suppressing myself, I have to get real about my feelings and what I want.

I thought helping people made me powerful. Loving others made me feel good. Helping people and loving others is a good way to be, but it was the way I was doing it that caused me harm, which increased my shame, and fed my addiction.

At one point in my bodywork career, I was doing very well professionally, but in my personal life I was on a downward spiral. Helping people was the only thing that made me feel good, which meant that when I wasn't helping people, I felt bad.

I worked long hours doing bodywork and then went home worked long hours on a failing marriage. My health was bad, I looked and felt like hell, but my business was going strong. I was helping people, they "needed" me. I couldn't quit and take a vacation.

It all came to a dramatic conclusion when my arm went out, I slipped and injured my spine, and my husband left me with all of our affairs in a mess for me to clean up. Suddenly I realized, I had been doing this all my life. I had to get real with myself about what I was doing to create this kind of scenario, and when I got real, I got better.

I found that I worked well with some clients and not with others. I started selecting my clients and cut back my work load. I began to enjoy my work more. I improved my communication in my relationships and started stating what I wanted instead of asking "nicely." All issues were dealt with immediately, no one got to hold onto anything and pout. No one had to be happy and nice all the time either. Suddenly there was more freedom to just be myself with people.

There are many groups that help people with addictions. In my area (Marin County) there are a lot of groups for Women Who Love Too Much, Alcoholics Anonymous, Codependents Anonymous, Narcotics Anonymous, etc. I have found going to support groups helpful. I've built up a network of friends I can call upon to share my feelings with when I am tempted to go back to old ways of doing things. If you feel you have an addiction you may benefit from joining one of these groups.

I went through the Huna purification process, which is based on the teachings of Max Freedom Long. It is a shamanistic process which recreates the personality so that rapport is established between the subconscious, superconscious, and conscious minds. It has some striking similarities to the 12-step program from the Alcoholics Anonymous program. Huna is derived from the teachings of the volcano kahunas of Hawaii. To learn more about it write:

Huna Research Inc.
1760 Anna St.
Cape Girardeau, MO 63701

The bibliography lists several books on Huna. Huna Kahunas teaching in the Bay Area are: Jack Gray (415)499-1860, Tom Stucker (415)927-HUNA, and Laura Yardley (415)381-2844.

Miscommunications and Crossed Wires

Many of our clients come into the session dealing with basic issues around love and survival. The interactions that we have with our clients are colored by these issues in subtle ways. The way we act toward them is a strong contrast to the way they are treated by the modern competitive world with its hard edges and dog-eat-dog attitudes, but our gestures and expressions are sometimes misinterpreted. For some, it is difficult to face the feelings of hurt, resentment, and emptiness that lie beneath the security of self-image. Usually there are painful memories associated with being loved. Under these circumstances, there are bound to be occasional miscommunications and misunderstandings.

One of the most common misinterpretations is **loving touch** getting transferred into the client's sexual needs. The emphasis our society puts upon sexuality, money, and power creates a psychic pressure to obtain these things "in order to be someone." The less obvious rewards of developing successful and meaningful love relationships, and the commitment to the process which does not guarantee instant solutions, instant sex, or instant love, is just not that apparent to some people.

Although our relationship with our client is in a professional context, we are touching their bodies, and this can be arousing despite the client's conscious intentions. This is often a secret embarrassment with men their first time on the table. If they comment on it, I try to make them comfortable by assuring them it is a common occurrence with relaxation.

Requests for sexual massage should be handled with the same consideration. You can be very direct without making them feel bad. The nicest people have asked me for a "complete" massage, but I know that it goes against my grain to accept money for sexual anything. There's no need to go into great detail with the client, I just tell them I don't do that and drop it. If they persist, I ask them this: "Would you go into an Italian restaurant and order Chinese food?" When they answer "no," I say, "Then why ask me to do that if it's not on the menu?" They usually laugh and drop it at that point. I've learned not to take these requests personally.

Suppose we are feeling something strained in our relationship with our client. We talk about it and we discover something we didn't know, a missing piece of information.

One time I thought my client was falling in love with me because he wanted to hug for such long periods of time. I questioned him about his home life very carefully, found nothing wrong there, but when we talked about his work life we found he was having problems with his boss.

This helped the two of us, therapist and client to move on. I wasn't there to fill that gap in his life, I was there to help him get in touch with himself so he could find a way to solve his problem with his work. If we hadn't talked about it, the feeling would have grown all out of proportion until it blew up in our faces, or in some cases, the client just stops coming.

Talking directly, honestly, and briefly is useful to the process. We're all human and deal with many of the same issues as our clients. The beauty of the transformative journey is that we get to be ourselves. The more real I am with my clients, the farther we get and the faster we go.

If we are feeling something unclear or off-center, we need to acknowledge that, or we risk losing a part of ourselves, an important part. We can learn how to grow beyond survival issues by confronting and going through them. In addition to having a lot of love, a bodyworker must have a personal fearlessness. We must be warriors on the path of the heart.

I should clarify that we don't want to let it all hang out, and show our clients our dirty laundry. I've suffered through too many sessions where I heard all about the bodyworker's problems and wondered why they weren't paying me for therapy.

All we need to address in our communication is the specific issue we have with our clients that is causing the problem. By admitting that we have feelings, we can make our clients more comfortable with their own humanity. Once again, it's finding that healthy balance.

Control Issues and Power Plays

For most of us, when a client doesn't get better despite our Herculean efforts, it seems like a form of holding out. It makes us a little crazy and causes our hearts to close down. We find ourselves using old unconscious strategies for getting what we want. Then what we are calling "healing" is not that at all, it's the negative use of power.

When this happens in a session, we might feel ourselves forcing the client to go somewhere they don't want to go. We may not be getting the results we expected, and in that frustrated state we feel we have to power our way through in order to get this person healed. We may be frustrated with our client's progress, frustrated with our technique, or their personality may have irritated us to the point that we just want to get them done with and out of our office.

We have to be sensitive to control issues. People use control when they are insecure about opening up themselves to love. We can be misled by a control issue and never get through to the love. Keeping the trust of

the person while we break the emotional armor requires a special skill. Like an acrobat balancing on a
tightrope while juggling fireballs, it's quite a trick.

One type of client who is likely to push our buttons
is the one wants to run the show. They will tell us what
to do, where to do it, and how they want it done. They
will compare us to previous massage therapists or
bodyworkers (usually unfavorably) and complain about
how much we charge.

Another way a client may try to keep control of the
session is to talk a lot. This is a distraction technique.
It keeps them safe from facing their key issues.

Others will put us in uncomfortable positions by
being needy: calling us repeatedly at all hours to
complain about their problems, telling us that they
need us to get well, yet are not responding to treatment,
the list is endless. The symptoms of these interactions
are: we end up feeling drained, angry, or just that we
compromised something in ourselves, but we don't
know where or when it happened.

People who do this are having a hard time. They are
using a power play because they're uncomfortable with
a feeling they haven't been able to express. But it won't
help them to go along with the power play. The session
is being used for something else than what it is
intended.

Often this type of manipulating leaves us feeling
irritable, tired, and confused, and these feelings can be
a warning sign for you of a power play. Most of these
people have no idea of what they are doing and direct
confrontation only creates antagonism. It's a Catch-22.
They have to be able to trust us before we can confront
them comfortably and they are not going to let us in
until we break through their defenses.

Most of these clients are not doing this because they

want to hurt us deliberately. They do it because they are afraid. Power plays are subconscious coping mechanisms which we learn when we are made to feel helpless, unloved or ashamed. They are survival mechanisms that worked once, they were adaptive. But they don't work in this situation.

To protect ourselves from the difficult client while we help them facilitate their healing process we have to recognize a power "tape" in progress, interrupt the program, and insert one that both of us are comfortable with.

The way we do this is to find a way to interrupt the program without tripping the alarm. First reflect upon their reality. Ask questions about what's going on inside. Match it as best you can, and start to gently lead them to a place where the mental energy can flow. For example, I was working on a woman's neck who was terrified of chiropractors. As she talked about having her neck cracked, the left side of her neck went into spasm and would not release. When I questioned her about what she felt there, she said it felt like a form of protection, like a leather band. I asked her to imagine the leather band inside her neck, and to move it just a little bit, a half an inch to the outside of her neck. The neck opened up and the leather band became a selective net that let my hands in.

It's important to avoid judging or patronizing these clients. Respect the innate wisdom of the body. We have to remember each person is doing the best they can, there may be factors keeping them where they are that we don't know about.

People in physical and emotional pain feel vulnerable; they are defending wounded places. There is a logical reason why they act that way.

Finding that logical reason is like being a detective,

it takes some careful research, a little deductive reasoning and a lot of intuition. Neither of you are in touch with why they are doing this, but the body knows. It is the medium through which the subconscious can communicate with you. Once that reason is acknowledged and addressed, it will be easy to get your client to relax and just let the healing process happen. It is important to act in ways that are clear, consistent, and helpful.

Being sensitive, truthful, and firm in our purpose will bring both of us to a good place. Often our clients look up to us a special authorities. But because of their past experiences with authorities, they may challenge us, needle us, give all their power away to us, or rebel against us.

With the aggressive, challenging client we need to be firm and not let ourselves be swayed by their way of interrelating to us. They are frequently locked into a perfectionistic mindset. The best part about being human is we don't have to know everything. If asked a question to which we don't know the answer, it is always best to say "I don't know. Would you like me to look it up?"

My most embarrassing moments in bodywork happened when I tried to answer clients' questions from my vast store of knowledge about the body, only to find out they were a doctor or other health specialist. Their position was that they knew more than me about that particular subject and wanted to test me. Even if I was knowledgeable on the subject, I subscribe to healing models they do not, and I was "proved" wrong. It can be frustrating to work with these people unless you know how to gain their trust.

We need to have a thorough knowledge of our field, and of the workings of the human mind. Gaining this knowledge is a process. We can take courses in psychology and read books, but the best way to learn is by observing people.

Dealing with difficult clients is one of the great challenges we face as bodyworkers. These relationships can be the ones that ultimately lead to the most growth for us, personally and professionally.

Growing along with my clients was always stimulating, sometimes exhausting, and motivated me to develop new ways of dealing with tough spots and tough clients. It strengthened my personality and helped me develop clarity in my communications, and when the breakthroughs came they were really exciting for both of us. Clear communication helped us focus our intent and energy on a common goal and built up a level of mutual trust. Both of us had been working very hard for the breakthrough and when the moment came, it felt wonderful!

Tools for Emotional Clearing

Here are some suggestions for developing and deepening emotional clarity. There are as many different ways to clear your emotions as there are to do bodywork. The criteria is the same as choosing a bodywork style: If it works for you, it's the best.

Body - Bodywork, cardiovascular exercise (running, swimming), body awareness meditation (zazen), internal martial arts (T'ai Chi, Pa Kua, etc.), yoga.

Mind - Meditation, therapy, journal writing, any creative effort focused on personal transformation, deep relaxation, yoga, mind games which improve imagination, intuition, and concentration, hypnosis and self-hypnosis, internal martial arts.

Soul - The spiritual path, approaching all events as a chance for personal growth, studying with a trustworthy teacher, reading and writing inspirational literature, retreats, vision quests, being close to nature.

Forgiveness or . . .
What to do when we don't feel sane

Not all diseases are physical. Some diseases are of the soul. The Sioux Indians have a term for this disease, they say "the heart is bad." I had a year when my heart was bad and I didn't feel like doing bodywork. Someone I loved very much wounded my spirit. I was grief-stricken and enraged, but after I disentangled myself from this person I went into a deep depression.

I was a mess and I knew it. It took a lot of time to get my heart clear because the hurt was so deep. Every day I worked at healing my heart, but it was a year before I started to feel like doing bodywork again.

My friends helped out tremendously. I never would have learned how deeply my friends cared for me and how much they were there for me, unless I allowed myself to be less than perfect...or together. I also learned the path of strength and forgiveness did not come from reciting spiritual platitudes, or "burning the wrongs done me in the violet flame of forgiveness." During this period of healing I burned through a lot of past rage by communicating my hurt to those who caused harm, and allowing them (if they wanted to) to make amends.

The communication with the parties involved was difficult to say the least, but allowing the pain to stay in my heart would have been even more painful. By going to the people who I felt wronged me, I had a chance to communicate with them about what they were going through at the time and understand why they did what they did. It gave them a chance to clear up their karma, so they don't have to recreate the same scene with someone else. They got a chance to understand me. Through understanding came compassion, and with compassion came forgiveness.

Even after the heart forgives, the mind may still run the angry tapes for a while. There were times when I had to tell my mind very strongly that I didn't want to dwell on the past, I was alive and free. I had a bright future and many things to be grateful for. I wanted to enjoy life now. Gradually, my subconscious got the message.

Forgiveness is the greatest quality a healer can have. It allows us to have compassion for the struggles of others. It keeps us from self-righteousness and pride.

I believe very strongly that what happens to us in life is not a measure of our merit, it's what we do with what happens to us that counts. For me it was not easy to forgive everything that happened. The consequences are still here with me today, but I am not a victim.

My life is better because I made it better. I couldn't wish the past away and I couldn't chant it away, no therapist could wave their magic wand and take the hurt away. Getting clear took effort, and time, and then more effort. It took me a long time to get emotionally strong again, but after it was all over, I felt like a phoenix that had risen from its own ashes. I felt powerful and alive, I had a wonderful love relationship, greater clarity in myself, and new directions in my career that were exciting and profitable. An interesting side benefit was that I had a lot less fear of everything. I had faced what I dreaded most and not only survived, but had come out a winner.

CHAPTER EIGHT

PSYCHIC SELF-CARE

This was the hardest chapter of the book to write. Most of my life I've been afraid to talk and write about the supernatural because to do so would be "unscientific." Much has been said and written on the subject by both skeptics and believers. I've devoted time and effort to both sides of research: I've worked as a parapsychology research assistant, studied and taught intuitive development, and trained with kahunas and medicine women. I've met and talked with some of the top people in the field. However, all my research did not make me a **believer** of the supernatural as much as it made me a better **user** of psychic abilities.

Most psychic research is focused on proving its existence and studying the conditions under which it is most likely to occur. I do not doubt these subtle forces exist, and these forces can be observed, felt, and directed by individuals who possess the innate ability and training. I habitually use these forces in my practice and my daily life, and have done so since I was a child.

I showed a peculiar sensitivity at a very young age; I saw halos of light and color around people and dancing lights moving through space in certain rooms. I kept my experiences a secret. Whenever I attempted to tell my friends and family about them, I was not validated. I learned that unless someone has had experience with these forces, they are not likely to know what to make of someone else's experiences. Some people out of ignorance, fear, or jealousy, told me I was crazy and mocked me. Later in life, I encountered other individuals with alternate reality experiences who supported me in coming out of the closet with my psychic abilities. Times have changed, and there is more support for and understanding of psychic awareness than when I was growing up.

I have since trained with several teachers, partly out of curiosity, and partly to gain some control over its unpredictable nature, and partly because it was necessary to learn to separate what was my own dream response and personal projection, and what I was truly sensing from others. As you can see, I am not a scientist, I am a student of this phenomenon. I leave the theoretics to the psychologists and the paraphysicists. I am more interested in the technology of these forces, i.e., how are they to be most wisely used?

The emotional issues around rational thinking and the supernatural are so heated that this prevents most people from just observing psychic phenomena, or giving adequate consideration to its practical and ethical implications. The following is simply my understanding of what psychic energy is based on my lifelong experience with it.*

I am only one individual and this is by no means the whole picture, because as the famous story goes, three blind men feeling an elephant will describe the elephant quite differently. The one feeling the trunk will say it is soft at the end and long. The one at the leg will say the elephant is big around and quite rough. And the one at the rear will think he has the answer to everything about elephants.

---

*A caution: teaching psychic awareness has taught me that this form of awareness is just as subjective as any other form of perception. Often my students would "read" the same person, come up with information that made sense to the person being read, and yet say entirely different things. All intuition should be treated as a perception, and not be given more weight or authority than any other sensory modality. An important concept in the technology of intuition is the different viewpoints of reality.

As I describe what I've observed and learned, please remember I'm like one of those blind men who can feel only one part of the elephant at a time. I will do my best to represent accurately my personal experience with the supernatural, and make no scientific claims about its existence or non-existence.

The Web

Surrounding our bodies and interpenetrating every cell is a network of fine lines through which a highly-refined form of energy flows, much like electricity flows through conductive wires. The flow of this energy follows thought—wherever we put our attention, that's where the energy goes.

We live in an interconnected Web of Reality which is composed of life energy and a composite awareness. Each of us is a nodal point of energy and awareness.

Modern science has attempted to capture and measure this energy, but so far without much success. The most delicate instrument in physics has difficulty detecting anything at all. However, research with living things: plants, rats, and people revealed a world of sensory interconnectedness that is not part of our physical senses.

We have a dual nature: although we are connected to all living things, we are also distinct entities. We have boundaries, but those boundaries are malleable. They are changing all the time because we are constantly changing what we think.

It is helpful to know what the boundaries between

all distinct entities in our environment are and respect them (have you ever walked into a glass door by accident? I have. It hurts, doesn't it?). We also need to recognize their transitory thought-constructed nature as well.

A few individuals can see these interconnections. Many more can feel them: experiencing heat, prickling sensations, cool breezes, or tingling when life energy moves through them or by them.

If you have not had a chance to experience what this feels like, don't be discouraged. Often it is a matter of where one puts one attention, and training that attention will improve the ability to sense energy.

This is one exercise that works for many people. *Hold your hands about a foot apart and imagine a ball of energy between them. Stay relaxed and keep your concentration on this ball until you feel pressure or heat growing in the palms of your hand. Try compressing the ball and see if you can feel it resist you. Now try making it growing by imagining it getting bigger.* Many people have great success with this experiment.

A way of experimenting with "seeing" this energy is to get a friend to stand or sit in front of blank white wall at sunset. As the light grows dimmer, relax and carry on a conversation. If you are not trying too hard, you may see a glow around their head and shoulders. This is glow is the **subtle energy body,** which surrounds and permeates the physical body. The size of the subtle energy body can be quite large or only a couple of inches beyond the boundaries of the physical body, depending on the degree of vitality and relaxation of the person you are viewing.

Another way to experience this is to watch someone who has been practicing T'ai Chi for many years do a set. They will leave "trails" behind as they move. This will work only if the person is relaxed and running a lot of "chi" (another word for life energy.)

It is through this web of interconnectedness that life energy flows in the healing session.

All parapsychologists have been able to prove so far is that we are interconnected in subtle ways which cannot be measured by physical instruments. These forces may not be physical, but they can be used to effect the behavior in living organisms. Psychic researchers have performed several experiments with different species in which two groups developed simultaneous behavior changes independent of each other. Rats became agitated when their companions were harmed, although both groups were separated by several floors. Plants reacted strongly when researchers tore or burned the leaf of altogether different plant in the next room. Paraphysics describes this phenomenon as **resonance**.

Resonance is a natural phenomenon. Children, dogs, cats, and plants all resonate with their environment, much like the strings on a violin will resonate harmonically with each other.

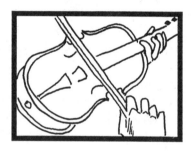

The stronger the emotional connection, the stronger this resonance phenomenon manifests itself. There are stories of people killed in war appearing quite vividly to loved ones at the time of their death and later the relative or spouse gets notification of their demise. Even in my very rational and science-oriented family there have been instances of telepathic communication between family members. If these studies indicate a true picture of reality then we are constantly exchanging energy with everything we come in contact with or think about, whether we want to or not.

The key phrase is "whether we want to." The difference between gaining and losing energy—the precious life force that ensures our health, survival, and intelligence—is choice.

"Cording" is a word used among psychics to describe this phenomenon. Cord is the word for the line of life-force energy that runs between two people. It is through the medium of this "cord" that energy is exchanged.

A possible explanation for this phenomenon comes from the kahunas of Hawaii. They believe that all living things have "aka" bodies (the etheric body of modern psychic science). The most outstanding quality of the aka body is that it is sticky and once it makes contact with something, it leaves an aka thread behind, much like a spider's thread. Mana (vital energy) flows along this thread, somewhat like electricity flowing through a wire, but it does not disperse in strength over a distance. The contact does not have to be physical, aka threads can be formed through viewing a drawing or a photograph, or just thinking a thought.

When in a session, some of our vital energy is being transferred into the client's body and some of their energy is being transferred into us via this contact. Early on in this book, we mentioned "taking on negative energy." Among the many past and present bodyworkers that I interviewed, one common reason mentioned of why bodyworkers quit was they could not avoid "taking on negative energy."

Although most cording happens on an unconscious level, we do have the power to choose who we cord with and for what purpose. This allows us a degree of

psychic immunity, the ability to resist psychic imbalance and disturbances.

It has been my experience that the techniques included in this book cannot guarantee absolute protection against negative energy. Only practicing the exercises with a determined, disciplined mind will yield results. The secret of success is not so much in which tool is used, but in the strength, abilities, and discipline of the worker.

The Psychic's Toolbox

Centering - Shutting out outside distractions and bringing the awareness into the self.

Grounding - Connecting with the earth's energies by constructing a mental picture of a grounding cord, or feeling roots growing down into the earth. Grounding is a powerful means of cleansing the subtle body of psychic toxins and debris, by mentally "sending" them down the grounding cord into the earth. For revitalization, imagine drawing up heat, energy and nourishment from the earth. I also use a technique in which I connect with my grandmothers, my female ancestors, and The Mother. The Mother has been known throughout history as the predominant feminine deity: Gaia, Athena, Kwan Yin, Virgin Mary, to name a few of her guises.

Cleansing - Using images of light, water, or fire to remove blocks and extraneous debris from the psychic environment and subtle body.

Decording - unplugging all people and situations that are draining your energy.

Exorcism - a stronger form of decording, for when someone is actually inhabiting a portion of your space and you need to evict them.

Shields - Visualizing energy shields that deflect and neutralize attacking energy.

Physical Aids

Crystals - A mineral body which composed of molecules which are arranged in a regular geometrical shape. Because of their ordered structures, crystals make good transmitters. They can also act as conductors for psychic energy. (It is important to realize that crystals and power objects can transmit good energy, bad energy, and too much energy. Caution is advised when using them. Frequent cleansing prevents transference of "static" to unsuspecting people, indiscriminate use can overwhelm blocked circuits and create imbalances in clients, and any use with other than the highest intention can harm the user.)

Power Objects - Any object worn on the person or used for ritual purposes that holds unusual amounts of mental energy. Can be used for protection, healing, and energy transference.

Herbs - Traditionally, one of the oldest materia medica of the world of magic and healing. Can be used ritually, burned as incense to expel negative energies, ingested to balance energies, heal wounds of all kinds, and induce altered states.

Bach Flowers - Potent essences of plants and herbs which help to heal "negative" personality states that would otherwise leave us too vulnerable to unwanted energies.

Supernatural Aides

Allies - Carlos Castenada with his titillating novels about his apprenticeship with Don Juan, a Yaqui Indian sorcerer, has popularized the idea of using allies. Allies can be great friends if understood, but can also be dangerous and demanding. Like power objects, it is important to know what you are doing when contacting an ally, and it is always best to be in the hands of an experienced teacher when doing so.

Guides - Teachers who communicate in dreams, visions, and through tools commonly associated with psychics, such as the Tarot, pendulums, automatic writing, readings from materials as diverse as bones, entrails, water, crystal balls, etc. It is advised to exercise caution with "channels." Just because someone is disembodied will not make them an expert on your reality. You're the expert on your reality. There have been several instances of malignant entities posing as guides. I have even sat in on some exorcisms of people who after consulting the "spirits" with Ouija boards and pendulums, developed aberrant and destructive behaviors. Remember this: You are the ultimate authority on your life. The best guide is your heart.

Power Animals - Meeting one's power animal is a rich, awesome, and a self-confrontational experience. Whenever I am about to make a big change, or have made a decision that is of high caliber, my power animal will show up to accompany me to the next level. The actual animal will appear, or some image, form, or sound representing the spirit of that animal will present itself and speak to me. I've worked with several over the years, but the first one was the eagle. The eagle is the one who sees far, the visionary.

Grounding Meditation

This is one of my favorite meditations for revitalizing. *Sit in a comfortable chair with your feet squarely planted on the ground. Clear your mind and breathe* deeply until you feel relaxed. Imagine roots growing from the base of your spine, down your legs and into the ground. Let them grow deep into the earth, as far as they will go. Allow all negativity to course down into the earth and be neutralized. Imagine nourishment coursing up the roots and into your body made receptive by emptying out the negativity. See the nourishment going up your spine and out your nerves to nourish and rejuvenate every cell of your body.

An alternative meditation—*Instead of imagining roots, imagine great tubes penetrating to the very core of the earth. Allow the negativity to go down to the center and burn up in the great heat. Then let lava course up the tubes, filling your body with heat, fire, and vitality.* Go ahead and be creative with the meditation. The correct image or feeling will come to you naturally. The main points to remember are:

1. Sit comfortably with feet planted on ground.
2. Relax.
3. Breathe.
4. Imagine, feel and sense a strong connection with the earth.
5. Let the negativity drain out of you.
6. Let the nourishment pour in.
7. Thank the earth for the exchange.

Shielding - After grounding, imagine energy surrounding your body. To strengthen and crystallize the image, it helps to give it a form: egg-shaped (to buffer and protect), a shield (to deflect), the bow of a ship (to cut through), whatever form is appropriate to the situation. I usually give it a color, bright white or green. Once you can clearly picture this energy, see if you can feel it surrounding you. Notice any internal changes. Then see if you can sense it. Do you feel a kind of pressure on the skin? The more modes of thought (visual, auditory, kinesthetic) you can use in creating this image, the more real and effective it will be.

One of my favorite shields is a green egg which allows clear vision, and attunes my interactions with others to my heart, which facilitates communication. Grounding the egg form and sending a cord up to your creative source (God, Allah, the Great Spirit) increases the effectiveness of the shield.

Decording

After grounding, visualize the person in the relationship you want to work on. See your connections as electric cords that can be plugged into or out of, as you wish. Begin pulling out the plugs. Give the cords back to the people involved, thank them for everything they've given you and tell them you need your space now.

A way to decord which is more final is to visualize cutting the cords with scissors, a sword or a knife. Be sure to give healing energy to the ends of the cords, it removes any remnants of hurt, harm, or guilt about the decording. The best thing is to give them back to the person involved and wrap them in green light. Visualize psychic band-aids.

You will find it difficult to decord certain people. There may be a connection that keeps you both incomplete with each other. You need to finalize the relationship, and close the door to further invasions. You can try talking with them to make or seek amends. Look at what connected you in the first place and disconnect your physical reality from theirs. A ritual in which you scream, shout, sing, or drum them out may be useful if they cannot be contacted physically. You may want to seek the aid of a spiritual advisor.

Exorcism

Although exorcism is often associated with demonic possession, on a milder level, sometimes people get in your space and you just want them out.

In my limited experience with demons and possession, the immunity of the possessed is a more important factor to the permanent success of any exorcism than the power of the exorcist. A good exorcist can usually expunge an evil spirit, but often there is a strong chance of "re-infection" if the possessed personality is not healed of the psychological wounds that drew the entity in the first place.

In the milder forms of possession, the same holds true. If you are psychically strong, it is harder for an invasive person to take up residence in your sphere of comfort. They are also less likely to be attracted to you.

There is a strong psychological element involved in possession and addressing that psychological element will often make the "victim" a less attractive host to the possessing entity. Psychic health and psychological health go hand in hand, so healing past wounds and maintaining a positive active outlook on life is the best guarantee against possession.

So that you could get another view of the "elephant," I have included an interview with a professional spiritual counselor from the Bay Area.

Rev. Miguel Franco is also a business consultant with a private practice in Marin County. He frequently counsels people in how to clear themselves and their businesses of negative psychic energy. This is an edited transcript of the interview I had with him:

I am originally from Sao Paulo, Brazil, which is a very spiritually active place. I have been consciously working on my personal growth since childhood. Along with my background in engineering and business, I incorporate a scientific approach to my work in psychic development and self awareness. I believe that joy and fulfillment can be manifested in the physical life through an understanding of energy and its effects on matter. In a car accident, I had a near-death experience that led me to become more aware of the ways I could create my own reality. The car accident brought me in touch with several physical therapists and bodyworkers, both in Brazil and the United States. During my healing process, I learned a great deal about healers and the way they use their energy in the session. I learned that we operate like a TV station, broadcasting and receiving information all the time through our physical bodies. Though we often identify with our bodies, we are not our bodies, just as television is not just transmitters, antennae, or tubes. They are the devices with which we send, receive and process information. The body is the form that our consciousness chooses to manifest itself through, just as the TV set is the form television uses to send its signals through.

To fully understand our lives we have to become aware of the information that we are sending and receiving because this information is responsible for what we are creating for ourselves. It tells us when it is time to get a job, create a relationship, or go to the beach. The information that we use to create our lives reflects our consciousness level.

When we interact with people we are interacting with their consciousness—sending, receiving, and processing information. If we are unable to recognize when we are receiving information inappropriate for our lives, we start to experience problems in the physical plane. This inappropriate information can manifest itself in different forms, i.e. stress, accidents, lack of fulfillment, anxiety, anger, power trips, frustration with work, difficult relationships, self doubt and so on.

Information is energy, so if you mix your energy with someone else's, you can experience someone else's life. Your information, or your life, is like a motion picture that is being projected on a screen and you are the director, creating scenes that are most appropriate for your own movie. But if another movie, from another director, is projected on your screen simultaneously, you can get confused about what you are seeing or experiencing in your life.

You have all the information that you need for a fulfilling life right now. Your spirit, or consciousness, knows what is best for your spiritual growth. But if we allow ourselves to mix our energy with others, we may disconnect from our source of information and momentarily get lost in our path.

When you are in tune with yourself, you become a powerful healer. Your life is clear of negative energy, or any other energy that is not in affinity with your purpose in life. By knowing your own energy, you automatically know when the information you are processing is yours or someone else's. This awareness brings clear vision into your life, an invaluable tool. With clear vision you can also help people by seeing or sensing their energy field (sometimes called aura) and provide them with valuable information. There are several ways to have your channels working right. To be in tune with yourself is to be in tune with your own energy, information, divine light, essence, Higher Self, soul, God—call it what you like. Due to the nature of bodywork, it is very easy to have healer/healee energies mixed up and when that happens watch out!

When you work with someone's body, you boost

the activity of their energy centers (called chakras in some systems) which are sending, receiving, and processing information. In most cases, the energy centers that deal with body information (the lower chakras) are activated, broadcasting information about survival, emotions, sexuality and ego issues. All this information (or energy) is floating around the room and in your energy field. If your aura has a similar energy (and we often do because we have similar needs and experiences), it can generate a magnetic attraction (like attracts like). If you are not aware of your own energy, you can attract your client's energy into your space, or aura.

This energy is not yours and contains information that is not appropriate to your life. The same thing can happen to your client. If either of you are not in control of your emotions, sexuality, and survival issues, the other party may pick up that energy and experience those feelings.

There is also the possibility of attracting another consciousness with a similar energy, and the room can become crowded with disembodied spirits trying to communicate or to control the session. They are like vampires, psychic vampires. Sometimes the person has an agreement with an obsessor entity, perhaps a guru, teacher, or a lover, from this lifetime or a past one, allowing the entity to control the body. All kinds of authority figures do this.

If you experience sexual anxiety or depression, if you lose your sense of humor, if your mind wanders or you suddenly experience a headache during a session there is a good chance that "vampires" are messing up the pictures in your energy field.

Some healers give themselves permission to be manipulated by other entities, so they can control their clients. They can cover up doing that kind of work with the name of healing, but they aren't healing people, they are manipulating people.

If the client gives up their seniority to this person a bond can be created. You can both become hooked with each other for no apparent reason. If both of you are willing to grow you can use this opportunity for a healing. By expressing what you are experiencing, you can bring into light the matching pictures or information that you have with your client and vice-versa. By seeing the energy, both of you have an opportunity to let go of the picture, or energize the beneficial one.

There are people, healers and healees, that consciously mix up energies for personal gain, for the purpose of controlling people. I assure you that there is no gain in doing this. You stop your growth, your own healing process if you manipulate people in this way.

We are constantly picking up someone else's energy. It is OK if you know your own energy, or who you are, so you can make a separation with any energy that is not in alignment with your spiritual growth or path.

Meditation and visualization are my favorite tools for keeping in touch with my own energy. Meditation helps me to obtain and process my own information. Visualization helps me to manifest the information and to protect my energy field against foreign energy.

When you incorporate these tools in your daily life, you create a safe healing space for yourself and others.

This is especially important if you are a healer, therapist, or bodyworker. This might be a good time to say something about drugs. Some people use drugs to access information or to become more sensitive to other people's energies during a session. The problem with that approach is that you usually leave your body to get this information, and in doing so, you let more foreign energy to come in your space. It becomes more and more difficult to find what you want, and you take more drugs to get more information. In a short while, your body contains everything but your own energy and information.

If you cannot control drugs in your life, please stay away from any healing activity. Heal yourself first. I find that life is the best drug on the market, and it's free. Let's share this "drug" and get high together!

A large percentage of bodyworkers and therapists are not aware of their energy and information. They don't protect themselves before, during, or after a session. It is very easy to do this—by grounding your energy and keeping it flowing through your body, you can protect your energy field. By using visualization, in less than five minutes, you can create a safe environment for yourself and your client before the session starts.

I feel that bodyworkers have a special mission in the evolution of the planet today. They have the power to bring awareness to a large number of people from all walks of life. They can bring a terrific healing touch to our lives and make being in a body more enjoyable. I hope you bodyworkers make good use of your hands and have fun with your lives!

Miguel Franco
BUSINESS CONSULTING & SPIRITUAL COUNSELING
53 A Cazneau Ave.
Sausalito, CA 94965
(415)332-0627

CHAPTER NINE

ABUNDANCE

Deep inside I am at peace and my life is rich.

Abundance Is to Satisfy One's Deepest Longing

Abundance is more than money, it's a way of life. If all we wanted in life was money, a career in financing or real estate would be a more direct route to wealth than bodywork. What if money was all we needed to be happy? Then our list of priorities would be shorter and our path linear.

Bodyworkers, as a rule, have complex motivations. Other things seem to matter more: health, relationship(s), learning new things, personal growth, the list goes on. Money is not usually the top of our priority list, it's only sharing space with the other things. Why? **All we really want is to feel good and be happy.** Money is the vehicle to, not the goal of abundance.

Let's assume we already have all the clients we can handle. We've read <u>The Seven Laws of Money</u>, listened to our Tony Robbins tapes, and we've taken all the prosperity workshops. Thanks to our visualizations and positive affirmations, our income has doubled. Now we have all the clientele we need, but...we still have a black hole in our checkbook that keeps eating away at our prosperity...and we're not sure that our relationship is exactly what we wanted...and if you'll excuse me now, my inner child is crying.

We know how hard it is to do everything we want without money: classes and workshops...$$$, health care and organic food...$$$, a nice house to live in...$$$, an office that reflects our sense of aesthet-ics...$$$.

If you are struggling with money issues, something is in the way. Whatever it is there's usually a good reason for it being there. Subconscious needs are hierarchical, and there are psychological needs that precede money. Most of us are seeking self-esteem, caring, touch, warmth, a good listener, and a parent substitute. Our first programs deal with satisfying the most basic drives: physical and emotional security. If our first programs are not being filled, the new, more mature programs will not operate as well.

Until we can look at that priority and deal with it lovingly, objectively, there will be a problem with money. Without enough money in our lives, we are going to have a hard time living the kind of life we want to live.

Shifting money to the top of the list without sacrificing the other things seems hard, but that is only because it is. Do it anyway.

There are four things to learn in order to become financially successful as a bodyworker.

1. **It's OK to hustle.** Learning marketing may not seem as important as learning the latest bodywork techniques, but our marketing expertise can make or break us as a business.

2. **It's OK to reach out to touch someone.** Making physical contact is supremely important to our business. The more we do it, the more we are comfortable with our touching. Do you remember the first time you ever did a massage? Do you remember how good it felt to make someone feel good too? This memory (or any wonderful memory

of massage) is a good thought to hold in mind when you are out marketing. It feels good to be touched. If you keep on touching others, your practice will grow.

3. **It's OK to work another job while you are building your dream career. You may have to do a little juggling to get it all to work.** Stan Russell, writer, lecturer, and marketing consultant, once said to me, "Having a part-time job while we build our clientele may be distracting and tiresome, but it also is a way of supporting ourselves while we get on with our life work. It takes time, energy, and effort to build up a clientele, but it's worth the effort. A sure sign of genius is someone who is willing to do anything they have to in order to do their work."

I was waiting on tables to support myself at the time, but I wanted to shift my income source to bodywork. I was having a hard time with my practice because the waitressing was so physically draining that I didn't have energy for my clients. In the hypnotherapy session, I opened my mind up to finding a creative solution. I switched jobs, and worked as a clown on weekends. Now I have lots of energy for my clients and feel more balanced and happy.

How to Talk to Your Mind So It Will Listen

Stan taught me the way we talk to our mind shapes the perception of our experiences. He also taught me how to talk to my mind so it would listen.

For example, I was struggling with feeling there was too much competition in the workshop marketplace. My original thought: "Everybody's already done every workshop I want to teach. (I proceeded to list several examples.) Look, I'm being reasonable. There's no place for me in this market."

Stan's response to me was: "Maja, you are completely unique, there's nobody in this whole universe exactly like you. Nobody has had your experiences, genetics, and education. Even if you had a twin, you'd still be different from them because that's your way. What you have to offer is your uniqueness. So when are you going to teach these workshops?"

When I stopped defeating myself before I even got started, I found I could get a lot accomplished. My passion and enthusiasm for doing my work is boundless—as long as I keep my mind on track. I know I'm **on track, on course** and **on time** when I have abundant feelings.

Powerful positive suggestions enable us to tap the energy in our emotional stockpiles. This is the source of power for genius, and makes this kind of mind unstoppable. It's not that genius never fails. Genius does fail, like everybody else, but a true genius keeps on going **no matter what happens.** Success can be an obstacle for some, but for the genius, it's a relief. Financial success means being able to afford the equipment and having the time to do our work.

Rapid permanent changes occur if we use the fire of our enthusiasm wisely. Burned too quickly—like too much pine wood on a fire—it burns hot, and is out in a short time. But burned in an orderly progressive fashion, we will have a fire that will keep us hot for a long time. We will find how much we really need it to sustain us through waitress jobs, network meetings, licking endless stamps—whatever we have do to get to our success. For most, the path of the heart warrior is about overcoming obstacles to living our dream.

Warrior Mind

Becoming an entrepreneur/bodyworker is an adventure—it's not an appropriate occupation for the pussy-footed or the faint-hearted. Don't get hysterical when the economy goes sour and clients stop coming. Take that free time to get active on your promotion, and be more nurturing of yourself. You'll get results.

To struggle is not synonymous with suffering, a warrior's heart is filled with fear and joy and lust for a cause. Struggle is enlivening for a warrior.

My experience with most prosperity workshops is that they do not effect permanent change because they are based on magical thinking. **Magical thinking** is what children do, and works well in the moment, but it's hard to control. There's another kind of magic which is **applied mental discipline.** This kind of magic gets better results.

Building a massage or body therapy practice is a hero's journey. It will transform you if you persist. You will face overwhelming odds and intense passions. You will face internal and external shadows. It takes a strong will and an indefatigable courage that only a warrior with tremendous heart can bear.

The reality of being a healer/warrior is that it is not always fun. It's not always exciting. Joy is a part of it, but there's also ignorance and fear of intimacy to face, unassailable objections to move through, sexual innuendos and outright abuse, piles of sticky rancid sheets to wash, and uncertain incomes.

If we are warriors on our heart path, we face, embrace and make peace with our negative emotions. The emotions can get to you after a while, and the drudgery. We have the precious ability to make friends with shadows, that is our strength as healers.

Boredom, fatigue, irritation, and anger are not the walls that obstruct our growth, but are the doorways to greater self-knowing, compassion, and love.

Going through these doorways allows us to tap the source of our power to satisfy our longing for the most vital parts of ourselves. We have a deep passion inside of us driving us relentlessly—"Grow, grow, move now, don't hesitate, this is the moment..." This passionate yearning drives us when things look grim, and splashes perfume and color on our joy, making it all the more "in-joy-able."

If it is an adventure, it's a gamble, but our odds are good. We possess a stockpile of potential energy waiting to be used for just this purpose. Our emotional need for nurturance and restoration is expansive; we want to share loving touch with others. We possess in our touch, and our hearts and minds the richest, most fertile ground for the next step of human evolution. We are heroes of the light, piercing the darkness that threatens to engulf this earth, because we bring loving touch into the world.

It's a journey we won't regret, because it's a natural extension of our human capacity to survive, experience, and enjoy life. The most advanced portions of our brains are the seat of the nurturing behaviors which gave mammals the evolutionary advantage over dinosaurs. The reason why weak, squishy, furry little mammals could flourish during times of great geological change was because of their caring and adaptability, not because of their size or powerful muscles.

Like other mammals, we have our vulnerability and desire to adapt. The vulnerability is the key to having emotional richness, and the desire is what forces us to move and make decisions. We have a choice as to whether we live a life of vitality or to tread the well-trodden path of others. To live in technicolor, and experience all of the emotions, passions, desires we possess leads to a true abundance, a place of fullness and delight. Dr. Joan Nelson, MFCC, my favorite sex therapist, says it quite simply: "It's the lust for life."

The Nuts and Bolts

Enthusiasm and passion are a big part of making our business a success, but they are not the whole picture. I love to inspire others by actively practicing what I preach.

The most important part of action is knowing what to do, and then doing it. Planning so you always have a next step saves precious time and resources.

The nuts and bolts of building a successful massage or body therapy practice is making contact with potential clients and getting them on your table. It is a lot like building a bridge, you need a variety of structural pieces connected in all the right places. Otherwise, all you have is a lot of pieces. There is a logical order to build a bridge so the pieces fit together right, and there is an order to building a practice.

These are the steps you will need to take to build the bridge:

1. **Find your niche.** What makes your massage special? Who is going to want it? How are you going to contact these people? Are you going to rely on person-to-person contact; word-of-mouth; passing out your business card to merchants and businesses; advertisements (classified or display); posting flyers in health food stores, laundromats, supermarkets, or anywhere you find a bulletin board; signs on busy streets; setting up a table at street fairs, sports events, expos; going into hospitals to massage bed-ridden patients; con-

tracting with businesses for their stress reduction programs; public speaking?

2. **Practice your rap.** Whether you are at a party, or on the phone to a potential client, you should be able tc tell them exactly what you do and how they are going to benefit from you (and only you) in 30 seconds. After that, you've already lost 90% of the people. Here's my rap: "I do a combination of eight different massage styles which I call Neurosomatics. This bodywork style specifically addresses the causes of muscular strain and releases the nerves so they can function more efficiently. My specialty is neck and shoulder tension, do you have neck and shoulder tension?"

3. **Get the best promotional materials you can afford.** People are more likely to trust you with their body and their money if your promo looks professional. Invest in typesetting, graphic design, and *use big numbers for the phone number so people can read it without their glasses.* Someone may be having a migraine while they are dialing you.

A photo of you tells people a lot about you. You don't have to be beautiful to take advantage of a photo business card; you just have to look trustworthy. I have a friend who is facially disfigured because of a congenital birth defect. He has a face you'll never forget, and he uses it to his advantage on his card.

If you are just starting out, and don't have hundreds to spend, Walter Drake & Sons has photo business cards for about five dollars. Allow at least six weeks for your order. Their address is:

Walter Drake & Sons
12 Drake Building
Colorado Springs, CO 80940
(719)596-3854

Other types of promotional items you can invest in:

- Postcards (good for staying in touch with clients)
- Pens printed with your name, what you do, and phone number
- Kitchen magnets (magnetic material printed like paper).

Flyers are useful for posting, but nobody much saves them. Look for items people will save: business cards, pens, reflexology charts, etc.

The brochure is in a category by itself and its design is a little more complicated. The most important items in any brochure (no matter what your business) are:

Outside:	Title and Logo
	Tag line
	Your name
	What you do
Inside:	Description of your work
	How it works
	Benefits
	Testimonials
Right panel:	Biography and picture
	How to get in touch with you

While you are writing your text, think of how your work will feel to the client—will they be free of pain, more relaxed, connected? Use concrete terms, avoid New Age amorphisms. Make sure it is a kinesthetic visual description of your work, using graphic and literal words. The client has to be able to see it and feel it working for them.

This is the form I used for my first brochure. Since then I've learned a lot more about what makes a successful brochure from taking "The Personal Business Brochure" workshop from Ellen Looyen. She taught me the importance of making my brochure personal, so the client really gets to know me better. The workshop is designed to take you through a very thorough process. Weeks before I took the workshop, I received an exercise booklet in the mail. I sent out client questionnaires to see what my clients had to say about my work, I wrote a business purpose, a life story, a mission statement, a personal description...I had to work for my workshop! I loved it, and I loved what I got out of the process.

For example, here's my mission statement: "I believe the path to self-caring is through loving acceptance of ourselves, accurate knowledge of our strengths and weaknesses, and the integration of the deepest levels of our person with our highest ideals. I live my life for the joy of being alive and in a body. I love helping others get in touch with that joy."

My personal description:

I do wonderful things just for the fun of it—I clown for disadvantaged children, study stand-up comedy, I write passionate poetry and give it to someone who could use a little poetry. My favorite thing of all is to go to the beach and play in the waves with my dog.

When I looked at other brochures done by Ellen's clients, I was struck by the biographies and how they made me feel about the person.

Ellen Looyen knows the special needs of bodyworkers, and is willing to give you lots of helpful hints and resources to make a great brochure. The workshop is relatively inexpensive, and covers details you will need to know. Her address is:

The Personal Business Brochure
Ellen Looyen
P.O. Box 2098
Mill Valley, CA 94942
(415)388-9507

4. **Get support.** You'll need it. Join a support group of people who do what you do. Keep it separate from your marketing groups, so you can let your hair down about your feelings. Compare notes, techniques, business ideas. Go to therapy if you need to heal old wounds, trade if you can't afford it. Build a network of intimate friends you can call on the telephone when you need encouragement and support. Get together with them on a regular basis, for lunch, a hike, or to go to network meetings to make new contacts.

5. **Cultivate your clients.** People who know and love your work are more likely to come back. Sometimes they need to be reminded, it helps them take better care of themselves if you show you care. Call them up from time to time and ask them how they are doing. Be sincere, friendly, interested. Make them special offers. Send them announcements in the mail. Build a mailing list, keep it up-to-date and organized. And above all, keep in touch with the people you like to touch. They'll be able to feel the love coming from you, and appreciate you all the more.

6. **Save a portion of your income.** Having a financial cushion is much more important for entrepreneurs than most of us realize. Life is full of all kinds of surprises, everything from...taxes you didn't know about...to all your sheets wearing out at once. You may end up using your financial cushion for a much needed vacation, but having one is very important. My cushion varies from around $1500 to $5000 in a special savings account separate from my other investments. I will not touch that money unless I need to.

Lately, I've felt very full and abundant in my life. Partly because I've accomplished much of what I set out to do, but also because I have less to do. It wasn't always that way, I used to joke about my life and say I had a difficult adulthood. My life hasn't been as easy as I wanted to be, but I could say it's been an adventure in search of abundance. This is my story.

Money Is Fluid

Once upon a time when I felt really broke, I went for a walk by a stream. The stream was in a peaceful little canyon deeply-shaded by old pine trees. No one ever went there, so I knew I would be alone. I needed a quiet place to think. I felt **bad.** In fact, I felt so bad that I wanted to shoot myself in the head because I couldn't pay my bills, and I was too ashamed to tell my landlady I would be late with the rent.

I sat by the stream and let the sound of the water run over the rocks in my mind. As I dreamily watched the water trickling by, I found my gaze drawn to the wading pool just under the little waterfall. A realization seeped into my mind that no matter what the water did in any one locale in space, over time it always kept on rushing downstream. As long as there was water upstream, there would be a stream to flow downstream.

It dawned on me that this stream was a metaphor which I could use for money. Just as there were places in the stream where the water trickled, there were places in my life where money flowed too slowly for my needs. I also saw big places of money/water, where there was enough water/money to go swimming in. Those were my times of luxury. I saw times of water overflowing, bursting its boundaries, making new stream beds.

I realized that the stream depended upon the rainy season. In the spring, it would be gushing and full. The waterfalls would run, fish would spawn.

I realized that I was happy and in the moment when

my income flow was strong. I has the habit of basing my budget on what I thought my income should be, not what it was. Often, when I had a lot of clients, there would be a big gush of money, and it would take care of a lot of my financial problems that had been put on hold. But I couldn't count on it during a drought. When I needed reservoirs and streams of money, all I had was a trickle. There must be something I could do to change that, if only I knew what that "what" was.

Sitting there by the stream, the answer seemed very simple—all I had to do during my current financial drought was handle the situation, which I was perfectly capable of doing as long as I don't let myself get upset about things.

I had seen myself get upset about money too many times. When I am upset, I miss crucial dates, deadlines, personal cues, and come to abysmal conclusions. I wanted of a peaceful mind and to be calmly flowing like the stream.

It struck me clearly that I imposed too much anxiety upon my financial situation and did not apply enough gentle reasoning. **If I could gain control of my emotions, then I could gain control of my thoughts and finances.**

Seeing the stream as a metaphor for my own life gave me the hope and courage I needed. I went home and called my landlady, told her I couldn't pay the rent right now, but I would have it to her soon. In fact, I did come up with the rent that month; but more importantly I started to see money in a radical new way.

Freeing up my mind from savings accounts, paychecks, frozen assets, and boring dead end jobs allowed me to see the flow of money in my life, how I stopped it, how I could encourage more of it to come into my life.

I was hanging onto some old and inappropriate ideas about money. Some of them came from my family, some from my peers.

When I was a child and couldn't think things through for myself, I learned that no matter how much money you had, how big your house was, and the number of things which filled it—it was never enough. My parents **always** worried about money. I didn't understand why although there seemed to be plenty of everything.

Now I realize that my situation is different from theirs. They grew up in an era of scarcity. During the Depression very few people had enough, just surviving was a struggle.

I grew up in the Ken and Barbie Age when there was an excess of material things and a loss of spiritual value. I belonged to the hippie generation, where we flaunted our new-found poverty with colorful rags and a back to land movement that most of us flunked, because we couldn't stand the boredom and grind of poverty.

Both generations knew something was missing, but we attached different values to our objects and ideas about life. The results was tension between generations and within our own psyches.

My parents valued the good job. I valued meaningful work. They worked for big organizations. I usually worked for myself or at a grunt job that supported my meaningful work. They received money in the form of paychecks which did not vary, unless taxes went up or they got a raise. I got tips, commissions, compensations, contracts. Their employment was at affect of large impersonal organizations, mine was at affect of the marketplace.

Yet it was their advice, their voices, and their reality

which often occupied my subconscious thoughts. Meanwhile, my conscious mind was thinking something completely different because of all the workshops I'd taken, and the books I had read. The two parts of my mind were always at war with each other.

Sitting by the stream that day showed me that I needed very badly to make peace with myself. I had boxed myself in with my parents' attitudes about money so I would feel safe, even though I wasn't always comfortable. The discomfort of my situation was forcing me to look at those boxes and see whether they served me or not. The same discomfort caused me to examine some of my newly acquired attitudes from my New Age programming. I looked closely at the ways life would shake me up to make me want to throw away the boxes, or at least challenged me to make new better boxes. I felt a need to want to take more responsibility for what was going into those new boxes and make my life work for me.

I love my parents. They are my roots, and a good part of who I am comes from them. Yet I thought they had too much fear, and were over-concerned about money. I left them in a flurry of hippie rebelliousness, and made choices that led me to cut off my flow of money.

Since then I have learned there are other ways of seeing and approaching the world of money that are more productive and balanced than my parent's fearfulness, or my reckless romanticism.

Working with My Attitudes

Attitudes are crucial to empowerment. A negative attitude paralyzes action. A positive attitude allows the mind to tap emotional resources to get things done. I found that my biggest emotional block to a life of ease was a deep seated feeling of unworthiness and shame. I distrusted money because I felt it was somehow dirty and slimy. "Wash your hands after handling money, it has germs." I secretly sensed that it drained or corrupted you while you were trying to get it, because Dad was always so tired after work. When I bought what I wanted as a child I was shamed about the way I handled my money. I was given messages about money that made it seem an ugly necessity of life, like sex. "You have to do it, but you gotta make yourself do it. No matter how unpleasant the task, just grit your teeth and it will be over soon."

These thoughts are laughable now, but to a child's mind, these things are very serious.

Making money doing bodywork is one of the most wonderful tasks we've ever put our hands to. It's fun. It's satisfying work. We feel good about it. But how do we get through the unconscious blocks that impede us? How do we make a comfortable living doing it?

When we examine ourselves scrupulously with relation to money, we can discover and change those maladaptive attitudes for ones that do work. If we are having trouble with money, chances are good that there are subconscious attitudes blocking the flow of money.

Here are some of the negative choices I made in reaction to my parents' fears about money:

- Not to sell out like my parents did (cut off my roots)
- To avoid materialism at all costs (made me poor)
- Not to work too hard (made me bored)
- To have perfect freedom — no job, no family, no obligations (made me crazy)

I've worked hard to change these self-defeating attitudes. Here are some of the methods I've used.

Juggling

Jugglers are just about the funniest and most delightful people I've ever met. I joined a Sunday juggling group, and the ambience of fun, hanging out in the park and sunshine, plus the playful interactions with the kids and adults gave the whole experience a level of quality I'll never forget. It inspired me to create that quality in all levels of my life.

I wanted to know how I could do create that quality in my life with money. I decided to learn how to juggle with the idea of training my mind to think fluidly, like... how to let go of one thing so I had an empty hand to catch another.

I gave myself a series of lessons to learn.

1. **Dealing with rejection** - I started with the premise that no one really rejects another person, what they want is to continue with what they are doing. It's hard to feel or think about new things the head is full of serious thoughts. My object was to learn how to get more people to play with me.

I also wanted to learn how to give kindness without wanting anything in return, because that expectation discouraged me after a lot of "no's." I started throwing balls at people to throw back at me, to invite them to play. I learned that some will play with you, some won't. The ones that will are worth playing with. The others have something else they want to do, but I don't have to spin my gears trying to get them to play with me.

There are exceptions to this rule. When I see someone wants to play, but won't give themselves permission, then I give myself permission to explore their boundaries. I try to break through their resistance with an "Irresistible Invitation." I will let myself be the clown, which is to be vulnerable to be accepted or turned down.

What cured me of feeling rejected was learning how much I like to play. This is who I am, so I don't hang onto people who are not happy playing with me. I look for others who like to play with me. This makes for a lot of success in finding people who like to play.

2. **Receiving** - It was hard for me to learn how to hold out my hand to let the ball drop into it. I could snatch the ball out of the air just fine, but when I had to catch it, I was running all over the place and couldn't get past three throws. One, two, three...Luuunge (oops!)

I realized how easy it was for me to seize an opportunity, but how hard it was for me to receive a gift. I started to think about giving a lot and what it meant to me. I realized I wanted to do things more spontaneously, out of the blue, so I started to give people gifts for no reason at all except I wanted to. It helped me to accept more spontaneous gifts from others without wondering, "Why did they give that to me? What do they want?" When I learned to hold out an open hand for the ball to drop into, I also learned to say "yes, thank you."

3. **Emptiness** - From the empty hand, I learned to admit to having needs and desires. I learned I could ask to get them met. Learning to aim the ball so it flew in a consistent pattern and would drop into my open hand taught me to be specific in what I ask for.

4. **One thing at a time** - I worked at juggling for months before I learned to juggle with just one ball. It wasn't because I was stupid or slow, but because my ambitions were so big. It took a lot of retraining to get my hands and mind to think in a new way. But once I got the one ball down, two and three balls were easy.

The same applied to my businesses. The process of learning to juggle helped me to make up my mind about the direction I wanted to go with my career. I made the decision to let go of two things, the bodywork space I occupied and my New Age greeting card and novelty business, so I could focus on the third (the clown) and get it happening. It happened beautifully and bountifully. Then I went back to the other two and started experiencing success with them.

The balance between gravity and levity can be an effort and full of tension, or a dynamic dance of ideals, goals, and actions. Learning to juggle objects and money helped all areas of my life because it taught me the freedom to play. I found that I could learn smoothness and coordination when dealing with multiple variables by putting aside my expectations and allowing myself to be in a learning process.

While I was playing in the park with my juggling buddies, I learned many things about people, bodywork and marketing. The most important thing I learned however was that **what I wanted most from money was to be free to live a joyful, happy life**.

Now I am much more comfortable financially, and feel more abundant in my career and love life—all because I've learned how to "play" in life.

Celebration

Along with a better time, better people started to come into my life. Great friends and relationships, sources of support, and inspiration. I coined a new term to describe the type of people we were: Whoopies.

Well

   Happy

      Opulent

         Open

            Person

I choose for my friends people who are Whoopies. I learn from them, as role models, by deeply imprinting my mind with the good things I see. "I like that, I want to do more of that for people I like." I am fascinated with the process of what makes a Whoopie.

Whoopies have something special about them that sets them apart from the discontent—something which makes them quite remarkable.

I set out to discover what this mysterious "thing" might be. I hung out with people I adjudged were happy and successful. Many of these people, but not all of them, had a lot of money. They all seemed to have some "thing" in common however, and that was the quality of their life experience.
They expressed:

Enthusiasm and joyful motivation

Clarity of purpose

Focus and commitment

Self-love

Confidence

Gratitude

Faith in their process

While I was engaged in this process, I got a fortune cookie that said, "The precious qualities that you admire in your friends, are the qualities that reside in yourself."

I knew that if I looked for the seeds of what made people great, I could nurture and cultivate these qualities in myself. I knew that if I admired them, it was because I was developing a similar state. If I gave these qualities a place to live and breathe, these my own innate greatness would have a chance to evolve.

When I looked for these qualities in myself, I found them, waiting to burst out.

The process is not finished, I'm still learning about living more fully and the ways in which I can serve others. Each day, I get more focused and have a clearer picture about who I am, what I do, and the true sources of my living. *Abundance is a place of fullness. We cannot possess it, only be in it and enjoy.*

CHAPTER TEN

"Success" by Joycelyn Olivier

I've been doing bodywork so long the feel of success is second nature to me. I expect people to want my service. I know bodywork is invaluable and that it fulfills a lot of human needs, not just relaxation. But if you are just starting out you may be wondering: isn't massage just a luxury? Who will pay for something I just love to do? Who can afford massages, if I can't?

Anyone who has "good" hands and energy to give, has a gift to offer that people will want. If you find that your practice is not flourishing, spend time with someone whose practice is. Study people who are successful; find out how they do it. Inspire yourself as to what is possible. Let the feel of success rub off on you. Success in business is just another skill. You can learn it just like you learned your manual skills doing massage.

Even though I seem relaxed and casual about it, my practice is my business. I give it all the care and attention that any business person would give their business. I provide my clients with a unique service that they really appreciate and are willing to pay me well for.

As bodyworkers, we provide our clients with affirmative touch. This gives them a kinesthetic experience of their bodies that affects their internal organization as well as their outward structure.

Affirmative touch is an invaluable and indispensable form of feedback for the client's self-regulating system. It takes the person out of stress mode with all the hormones of fight and flight, and into rest mode. The rest mode has a biochemical environment which facilitates healing, immunity, and emotional equilibrium.

All forms of bodywork are valid in that you are helping your client to have a conversation with their body. The success of the session is less based on technique than on how well you can establish rapport with your client and have them feel their needs are being met. People are always responding to the non-verbal cues you radiate. I've observed this phenomenon consistently: if you are not sure of the value, you will hear considerations about how much it costs. You are totally in charge of how people receive your offering.

When you have energy to give, the phone rings and your appointment book is full. If you are distracted by emotional crises, depression, disorder in your life, or unconstructive beliefs, and expectations, no matter how much you need the money or how many promotional things you do to try to increase your client base, the dissipation of focus will influence the result. If you're considering a course in marketing, you might be wasting your time. Unless you have these other issues handled, they will influence the success of your venture.

Gaining Confidence

You should know the value of your work. Touching someone with loving hands can be as powerfully transformative as the most sophisticated of scientific techniques. The power of loving conscious attention changes people and the way their bodies respond to you.

You have a lot to give; I encourage you to know the value of your gift even during your training program. **The people you practice on receive value from your touch even if your technique is not yet great.**

Receiving payment for your work even as you begin, (no matter how much or how little), builds confidence in its value and begins to define in your mind and the minds of others as a professional—someone who receives money for a service rendered. One of the greatest stumbling blocks to getting started is seeing yourself in a new identity—"I'm no longer a secretary, carpenter, housekeeper, salesperson, I'm a massage professional!" Your confidence in the value of your work is what prospective clients will respond to.

Contrary to popular belief, there is no lack of bodies out there to be rubbed. If your appointment book is empty it is <u>not</u> because there are too many masseuses in your area. **There is no such thing as a saturated market for bodywork.** Everybody needs bodywork, but not all people know its value to them because they have never experienced it—or experienced you. Those in excellent shape need it to stay finely tuned and all the rest of us need it to support our intentions to feel better, live longer, look younger, and lead healthier lives.

Find Out What People Want

One of my clients has me focus for a full hour on just her face, neck, and hands. She says it works like a face lift. Indeed, when the tissues of the face are fuller and more relaxed, the eyes open wider, the brow unfurrows and the world looks bright again from inside and out.

I mention these details because someone you know may want to achieve these results with their face and not know it is possible. You don't need to make guarantees. One of my favorite phrases is "Let's make an appointment and see what we can do."

Mutual Support: The Open Hand Policy

There are people who believe that if you refer your clients to another practitioner you may lose them. For them this is probably true, since it reflects a lack of confidence in their own value and/or a sense of scarcity and a fear of loss.

I believe in giving and caring for people the best that I can. If they want a massage today and I'm not available I refer them to someone whose work is similar to mine. If I haven't worked with them before I take the time to find out what their needs are and connect them with the appropriate person. You may find it useful to develop an intentional reciprocal relationship with a colleague—someone who loves you and respects your work so that you can refer clients when you can't see them and they can do the same.

This open-handed approach is the best policy. It always pays. One of my dearest friends and a colleague also commutes like I do to the same large city to work. He is seldom there at the same time. I asked him once why he never referred his clients to me so they could get taken care of when he's not around. He was indignant, "What! Clients are *valuable*. People *sell* their client lists!"

This is not my attitude at all. Sometimes I wonder if this is not the reason why my practice is full and flourishing while his is sparse. I have another colleague in the same city who insists that all her clients come and see me when I'm in town, and I send her all my regulars too, when I'm not available. I want people to get the attention they need.

Establishing a Network of Referrals or...
Take a Chiropractor to Lunch

Other health professionals are in a position to send you lots of referrals, because you do something for their clients that supports and enhances their work. You may have to educate them to that fact. If they have received any training at all in marketing a private practice they will realize what a valuable resource you are also.

When you invite a chiropractor or other health professional to lunch remember that it is for your mutual benefit. It is not about you proving yourself. You may get a lot of resistance, you may have a hard time getting past the receptionist, it may seem like you have to prove yourself, but don't take that attitude. Massage and chiropractic belong together. You have something to offer that will benefit them. It's just a matter of getting to know each other's work so you both can feel confident making referrals. A successful chiropractor will respect your persistence especially if it's accompanied by a certainty of your worth.

You should make several of these connections around your health professional community. Make friends with chiropractors, a couple of holistic doctors, a homeopath, nutritionist, colon therapists, acupuncturists, orthopedic surgeons, exercise physiologists, weight trainers, salon owners, etc.

To take the best advantage of your lunch with another health professional, you first need to know something about the skills of rapport. Rapport is creating the feeling of oneness with another, the identification that you are one of them.

How do you get through to a busy chiropractor, doctor, or acupuncturist? Persistence. Plain old persistence.

First, compose a brief letter of introduction. If your resume is impressive, include that. Most chiropractors are not looking for someone with enormous skills or experience. They don't pay enough to attract those kind of practitioners generally.

Ask for something specific:

- Can I take you to lunch to get to know your work?
- I'm looking to establish relationships in the community of H.P.'s I might refer my clients to.
- I'd like to stop by your office for a few minutes so we might talk.
- I'd like to offer you twenty minutes of my work—I'd like you to know what I do.

When offering a busy health professional a sample of your work it may be best to limit it to 1/2 hour so they won't feel they're giving a big chunk of their time to something they're not sure they will like.

Second, call on the phone, find out if there is a considerate time to stop by.

Third, stop by right at lunch time—make friends with the receptionist or secretary while the doctor finishes with patients. The doctor's support staff can be important allies and spokesperson on your behalf. Keep all your doors open.

Where Does Your Business Come From?

Everywhere. Initially most of your business will come from your own circle of friends, loved ones, and their circle of friends and loved ones.

This is a wonderful way to do it because you've probably introducing a whole new group to the benefits and pleasures of massage! One of the things I love the most about massage is that the therapeutic technique is totally pleasurable. It is unique as a health enhancing modality for that reason. It is also motivational. It can help overcome the inertia most people have to taking care of themselves through good diet and exercise.

Your Rap

I can't really say that what I do is massage anymore. In fact, it probably hasn't been for a long time, but I described it as such. People are at least familiar with the term so their initial response is comprehension even if they still don't know what I do. In talking to people you need to find a way to describe your work that:

1. Puts you and your unique character in it (that may be simply communicated by your tone of voice for instance)
2. Allows your listener to immediately see the benefits to them.

Learning how to communicate is an essential aspect of bodywork as an entrepreneurial profession. The market of bodywork is brand new. It has never been developed. You are a pioneer in the field. In order to succeed you must educate a public. This could be considered difficult or challenging—not unlike some of the other skills you've already mastered in your course of study.

The first step is your rap.

Two pointers to remember:

- Make it short; don't attempt to extol all the virtues of bodywork in one paragraph. There are too many of them.

- Be willing to accept the challenge of describing what is essentially a non-verbal experience. Your attitude communicates vast amounts about you and your work. Don't be superior about your knowledge. Share it willingly. Resist the temptation to get clients by "hexing"; telling them what's wrong with them or their posture/structure. Ask questions as soon as possible in order that your answer can be specific to their needs. Talk more about the benefits to them than about the features of your work.

I know you'd like me to say more about how to talk to people about your work. "With confidence" is the phrase that keeps coming back to mind. That is the most telling component of your verbal presentation. The basics of your verbal presentation should contain:

1. Your name (if your audience of one or more people don't already know it.
2. What you do.
3. What's unique about what you do. Either something unique to your style or to the experience they will have with you.
4. What the benefits will be to the person who receives your work.
5. Use of body language, tone of voice, and intentionality to communicate the quality of the experience

they will have in your presence. Your body is the best advertisement for what your work does and is about.

6. If appropriate, you might want to get more specific and say where you work, how long your sessions take, and how much they cost.

Generally, if someone asks you "what do you do?" you will have about thirty seconds of their time before their attention begins to lapse. Unless you are talking about them of course. So after giving someone a 30 second synopsis of the most salient points about your work, it is better to continue the conversation by directing questions about them that will give you information about how you can be of service and reveal to them how well their needs might be met by sampling your work. For example:

I'm Dorothy Rosas, and I'm a Feldenkrais practitioner. In my work I use my hands to guide your body into gentle repositionings and manipulations to re-educate your muscles and nerves, to help them be more comfortable and work more harmoniously together. Did you know you can change your body posture and repattern your nervous system? Tension patterns and pains can disappear. This technique has helped people with arthritis regain use of their joints. Have you ever had painful tension patterns arise in your body? You have? What brought them on? Was it something you were doing? Feeling? Stress? Do you get them often?

Get personal as soon as possible. Show people you're interested in them. Ask questions. People love to talk about themselves.

The example I've given you is more of a formal presentation to an individual. You can modify the questions to address a group also. eg. *Has anyone here ever had low back pain? Recently? Does it recur? Well, this work can help you tremendously. After five or six sessions some people become totally free of back pain. And, should it recur sometime in the future you'll have all the techniques you can use yourself to relieve it. We take time to teach you subtle movements or exercises you can do to reinforce the work we do in sessions.*

How Do I Generate Rapport?

How you talk to people is of utmost importance—even after they are on your table. Very quickly I learned in doing massage that many people are looking for what's wrong with them so they can fix it, worry about it, etc. They will invite you to tell them about whatever you find going on there. This is simply a continuation of a negative self regard fostered by the critical conditioning of parents and peers.

I **will** tell someone about what I find, but I look for a way to say it so it empowers them or creates a positive framework for understanding and/or transcending the nature of the condition. Bodywork is a constant communication of new information to the body and brain of both recipient and giver whether you speak or not. Your knowledge of bodies communicates/translates directly from your hands to their body. Because of this, the more you know about anatomy, physiology, energy, and technique, the more enhanced is your intuitive rapport with the body. However, technique and knowledge only enhance the primary power of loving conscious attention, they cannot substitute.

Don't feel obliged to tell someone everything wrong with them that you find. I've never noticed the activation of critical regard to be conducive to the healing process, usually it is the cause of the process of disease.

Some people scare clients into thinking they've got to have more work. I prefer to encourage people by reminding them what wonderful experiences are in store living in a finely tuned temple.

- Be comfortable with yourself. Years ago I realized that all I needed to do for people to be comfortable around me was to feel comfortable about myself. It was a great revelation at the time. I used to be very nervous around strangers.
- Speak in similar tones, words, and rates of speech as the person you're speaking with.
- Validate that other person's experience. Let them know you can understand their perceptions and feelings.
- Make statements or ask questions they can say "yes" to, eg. You probably have tightness when you are so tired. It would be nice if someone else could take over and take care of you. Or...do you ever have places on your body that hurt or ache from time to time?

I have a girlfriend I used to trade bodywork sessions with. When she came across knots and tight spots in my body she'd say, "O-o-o-oh ca-ca!" (a baby's first word for shit). I didn't appreciate being talked to like that. My muscles know that they are working as hard as they can to carry loads I ask of them. They'd like appreciation, not criticism. They respond to acceptance plus invitation, not condemnation.

The physical body's emotional sensitivities are very childlike. Its feelings are hurt very easily. I've even seen it happen in a classroom situation where professional bodyworkers were learning a new skill, muscle testing.

Two people were coming to angry words because one of them said, "You <u>should</u> test stronger than this!"

I give bodies and psyches lots and lots of acknowledgment for what they're doing right and for each little improvement. Even though you may feel awkward at first giving this kind of verbal feedback the body will respond to it. When you ask someone to breathe into your pressure and they try it say, "Good, good." If they didn't get as much response as you thought possible, repeat your instructions with more specific directions so they can refine what they are doing. Don't waste time telling them it wasn't quite right. It's easier to build on success than failure.

You may be wondering what this has to do with establishing clientele. Everything. Even when clients don't consciously know why they are responding to you in a certain way, unconsciously they are reacting to the messages you're putting out. This is why it serves you to learn as much about the magic of rapport as you can so that you can talk to people's unconscious and create comfort for your clients. People will love to be around you. Then you'll have a new problem—how can I possibly serve all these clients without wearing myself out? For the answer to that, you can read this book.

BIBLIOGRAPHY

Bailey, Alice. Glamour: A World Problem. New York: Lucis Publishing Co., 1978.

Beattie, Melody. Codependent No More. USA: Hazelden Foundation, 1987.

Benson, M.D., Herbert, The Relaxation Response. New York: Avon Books, 1975.

Bettleheim, Bruno. The Uses of Enchantment: the Meaning and Importance of Fairy Tales. New York: Random House, a Vintage Press Book, 1977.

Bird, Christopher and Tompkins, Peter. Secret Life of Plants. New York: Harper & Row, 1973.

Brennan, Barbara Ann. Hands of Light: A Guide to Healing through the Human Energy Field. New York: Bantam Books, 1987.

Buscaglia, Leo. Love. New York: Fawcett Press, 1972.

Campbell, Joseph, ed. The Portable Jung. New York: The Viking Press, Inc., 1971.

Cassidy, John and Rimbeaux, B.C., Juggling for the Complete Klutz. Palo Alto, CA: Klutz Press, 1988.

Castenada, Carlos. The Eagle's Gift. New York: Pocket Books (division of Simon & Schuster), 1981.

Chang, Dr. Stephen T., The Complete System of Self-Healing: Internal Exercises. San Francisco: Tao Publishing, 1986.

Cox, Connie and Evatt, Cris. Simply Organized! New York: Perigee Books, 1988.

Fabun, Don. The Dynamics of Change. Englewood Cliffs, NJ: Prentice-Hall, Inc., 1970.

Gaylin, Williard. Caring. New York: Avon Books, 1976.

Graves, Tom. Needles of Stone Revisited. Glastonbury: Gothic Images Publications, 1986.

Jung, Carl. The Portable Jung. New York: Penguin Books, 1976.

Keleman, Steve. Emotional Anatomy. Berkeley, CA: Center Press, 1985.

King, Serge. Mastering Your Hidden Self: A Guide to the Huna Way. Wheaton, IL: The Theosophical Publishing House, 1985.

Kubler-Ross, Elisabeth. Death: The Final Stage of Growth. Englewood Cliffs, NJ: Prentice Hall, 1975.

Laut, Phil. Money Is My Friend. Cincinnati, OH: Trinity Publications, 1986.

Long, Max F. Recovering the Ancient Magic. Cape Girardeau, MO: Huna Press, 1978.

Long, Max F. Secret Science at Work. Marina del Rey, CA: DeVorss & Co., 1953.

Long, Max F. Secret Science Behind Miracles. Marina del Rey, CA: DeVorss & Co., 1976.

Miller, Joy and Ripper, Marianne. Following the Yellow Brick Road: The Adult Child's Journey through Oz. Deerfield Beach, FL: Heath Communications, Inc., 1988.

Millman, Dan. The Way of the Peaceful Warrior. Tiburon, CA: H.J. Kramer Inc., 1985.

Mishlove, Jeffrey. The Roots of Consciousness: Psychic Liberation through History, Science, and Experience. New York: Random House, 1975.

Rolf, Ph.D. Ida. Rolfing: The Integration of Human Structures. New York: Harper & Row., 1977.

Russell, Ph.D. Stanley E. Rapid Personal Growth. Sausalito, CA: Russell Dynamics, Inc., 1988.

Sasz, Tom. The Second Sin. Garden City, NY: Anchor Books, 1975.

Scarf, Maggie. Unfinished Business: Pressure Points in the Lives of Women. New York: Doubleday & Co., Inc., 1980.

Soho, Takuan. The Unfettered Mind. Tokyo: Kodansha International, 1986.

Tulka, Tarthang. Time, Space, and Knowledge. Emeryville, CA: Dharma Publishing, 1977.

Tohei, Koichi. Book of Ki: Co-ordinating Mind and Body in Daily Life. Tokyo: Japan Publications, Inc., 1976.

NOTES

NOTES

NOTES

NOTES

NOTES

NOTES